Life Literacy

Advance Praise for Life Literacy

"Every Human Resource and business leader needs to read this book! *Life Literacy* will teach you how to hire the right people and create a culture that will allow your business to thrive."

Marshall Goldsmith, *New York Times* No. 1 bestselling author of *Triggers, Mojo*, and *What Got You Here Won't Get You There*

"Every single student and adult will learn actionable lessons in Life Literacy. It's not a book of rules, it's a book that shines the light on our everyday reality with all bases covered. A must read, I will be sharing this with my kids, friends, clients, and anyone else who wants to avoid making the mistakes that many of us make each and every day."

Nick Roud, Co-Founder & CEO, Roud Career Coaching, New Zealand's No. 1 Executive Coach 2020

"Achievers know that accountability is the foundation of all success. Champions commit to doing what's right, following through, and making good on their word. Matt, Nelson, and Stan wonderfully articulate the disconnect facing our society today, and what it will take to get us back on track. Whether you are an executive, entrepreneur, parent, teacher, coach—or teenager about to embark on your life's journey—Life Literacy is a must-read to achieve your personal and professional goals."

John G. Miller, author of *QBQ! The Question Behind the Question* and *Raising Accountable Kids*

"As first glance this book is perfectly positioned to hand to every student one year away from graduation to help them decide where to start their career and get off on the right foot. But actually, it is relevant for any professional as a 'reminder' of how to manage your 'whole self' as you navigate your career. And as a leader it is important to keep in mind how you lead your team, as it is as important as ever that we lead and care for our team rather than just manage the outcomes. Really inspirational!"

Summer Smith, Vice President Talent, Diversity & Inclusion, and Capability at Rolls Royce

"The skills to succeed in the world of sports are no different than those required in any other discipline. Matt Young, Nelson Soh, and Stan Peake expertly articulate how essential it is for anyone to have a clear and compelling purpose, values that drive their behaviour, and a set of skills and disciplined personal practices to set any professional up for success. Life Literacy belongs on the must-read list for anyone serious about becoming a success in their chosen endeavour, be it accounting, leadership, or coaching the worlds' top athletes."

Michael O'Donnell, Senior Director of Player Development, PGA

"As a radio presenter coach, I spend a lot of time listening! Not just to clients but their work output... their radio shows. Sometimes, when we do something so often and with such repetition, it can become automatic. I loved the way this book clarified the Three Levels of Listening. From my perspective, understanding that Level 3 Listening outdoes effective speaking every time was both an eye-opener and a revelation. A real 'Aha' moment... and there are many, many more in this book."

Nails Mahoney, OnAirCoach, Malta/London, TEDx speaker, and host of Radio Star global talent search

Real Life KNOWLEDGE and
RESOURCES for the NEXT GENERATION
TO SUCCEED

MATT NELSON STAN
YOUNG SOH PEAKE

NEW YORK

LONDON • NASHVILLE • MELBOURNE • VANCOUVER

Life Literacy

Real Life Knowledge and Resources for
the Next Generation to Succeed

Published in New York, New York, by Morgan James Publishing. Morgan James is a trademark of Morgan James, LLC. www.MorganJamesPublishing.com

Morgan James BOGO™

A **FREE** ebook edition is available for you
or a friend with the purchase of this print book.

CLEARLY SIGN YOUR NAME ABOVE

Instructions to claim your free ebook edition:
1. Visit MorganJamesBOGO.com
2. Sign your name CLEARLY in the space above
3. Complete the form and submit a photo
   of this entire page
4. You or your friend can download the ebook
   to your preferred device

ISBN 9781631953866 paperback
ISBN 9781631953873 eBook
ISBN 9781631953880 audio
Library of Congress Control Number:
2020948954

Cover Design by:
Christopher Kirk
www.GFSstudio.com

Interior Design by:
Chris Treccani
www.3dogcreative.net

Morgan James is a proud partner of Habitat for Humanity Peninsula
and Greater Williamsburg. Partners in building since 2006.

Get involved today! Visit
MorganJamesPublishing.com/giving-back

For every contributor, every trailblazer, every mentor. For every team player who understands they have a part to play, rather than something owed to them. For those who are willing to sacrifice for the betterment of the whole, and for those leading from a place of service rather than title—we wrote this book for you. May you be the change that you wish to see in the world. May this book act as but a spark to light your fire that goes on to inspire the world!

Table of Contents

Chapter One

A Dream Turned Nightmare

t was 1995 and we were just about ready to graduate from college. It was crunch time. We'd spent years in the theoretical world imagining the perfect career. And now we needed to decide what we would do in the real world to make it a reality. Few of our classmates knew what their next career step would be. Not us though, we knew exactly what we wanted to do.

We were going to be the first of a new breed of personal trainers. No, not the celebrity kind on the infomercials all over late-night television—the ones with the impossibly white teeth, six-pack abs and orange skin. It seemed like there were already too many of them! We'd been researching the personal training industry for years and found an unrealized gap. It was a gap that presented a massive opportunity for us to do more than just transform people's bodies. We wanted to transform their lives.

The sector was new, immature, and unregulated. And since it wasn't mainstream yet, we felt like mavericks. We had the opportunity to create life-long changes for clients; ones that they'd never forget, ones that had more to do with their insides than outsides. We were excited to get rolling.

As two novice entrepreneurs, we spent our final semester of school honing our business plan. Ensuring we knew our target market inside and out. With our plan in hand, we briefly went our separate ways to pay our last respects to the lives we'd been living before school. It was now time to buckle down. We loaded up our belongings and drove across the country to set up shop. Our timing turned out to be perfect. One of the clubs that we'd formerly worked at just went under. Everyone was looking for somebody to train them. We took over the business and put our sports backgrounds and team mentality to work!

We were firm but fair with clients, and pursued our day-to-day work with a relentless passion. In those early days, I think it was more important to *us* to get results than it was for the people we trained. We were testing theories and trying new tools. And man, did those clients ever appreciate what we were bringing to the table! They'd never seen anything like it. We had people doing crazy, unorthodox things. We were all about pushing people as far outside their comfort zones as possible.

Our rationale was simple: There are five spheres that comprise the most important things in people's lives. The physical, spiritual, social, emotional ,and intellectual spheres (Fig 1.1.). Ninety-nine per cent of personal trainers were focused on the physical, specifically weight training, so we didn't have to reach too far in order to differentiate ourselves from the rest of the pack. But simply being different wasn't good enough for us. We didn't want to be anywhere near the pack. We had energy, passion, and we brought fire to every session. To be honest, the work was bigger than just us. We loved watching people stripped bare of their social masks. It didn't matter how much money they had or what they did for a living. We wanted nothing from them other than the privilege of watching them react to the adversity bestowed on them by our challenges. I remember a 76-year-old man who wet himself with excitement 500 feet from the summit in Kilimanjaro, tears of joy in his eyes that he'd accomplished something so profound. It was heady stuff. We demanded 100 per cent from our clients in every session. We challenged them to commit to the process and promised them they'd find something new inside themselves. They always did.

In those days, there was no Internet, iPhone or social media. It was mano a mano, and we followed up with actual phone calls every day.

Fig 1.1: The Five Spheres of Human Development
Photo credit Innovative Fitness.

Unbeknownst to us at the time, what we had created was a conduit to connection. This was an important part of our process but I think the biggest X factor was genuinely caring for people's well-being. And it showed. We weren't about losing 10 pounds or getting a firmer chest or adding inches to biceps. We were about helping people accomplish things they'd always wanted to, but didn't think they could. Or knocking something off their bucket list they'd never prioritized in the health and fitness realm.

We ran alongside people for 5ks, 10ks, 1/2 marathons, marathons, duathlons, triathlons, and Ironmans. We jumped out of planes skydiving, off bridges bungee-jumping, moto-ed down the Baja 1000! We hiked the Grand Canyon, across Iceland, Machu Picchu, Mt. Rainier, Mt. Kilimanjaro, and even ran across the Sahara desert. If an idea fell out of someone's mouth, we were registering, training, travelling, and doing it. This wasn't a job, it was a privilege.

We quickly established ourselves as *the* go-to training company in the city. People saw our work ethic and admired our passion, commitment and drive. There was nothing like us in the industry. We cooked people's meals, listened to their personal problems and helped them with their businesses. I remember listening to a woman muster the courage to leave her family business to branch out on her own. She had a unique concept but was lacking confidence. We mapped out the business plan, the exit strategy, all of it. At the 11th hour she wanted to back out and we nudged her off the ledge. She turned her little idea into a multi-million-dollar business—*and* got in the best shape of her life.

We were giving people the tools to meet their dreams. We were actually changing people's lives and loved our jobs. We were growing and needed to decide what was next. Where should we go from here? We sat down with our financial advisor and he asked us where we ultimately wanted to end up. Our answer was in Vancouver, British Columbia because there was nothing like this there. No competition, fertile ground that was ripe for growth. He suggested one of us stay behind while the other went to test the waters. So we went our separate ways. We set up shop in two cities and each worked 24/7. The risk paid off. Within six months, we were so busy we needed to hire more people in order to continue to scale. We were careful building our team, so we mostly brought on friends and college classmates, people who found our enthusiasm infectious.

Now it may sound like it was all roses but we all know starting a business isn't for the faint of heart. The challenges never stop coming at you. It becomes really obvious at some point that you don't know what you don't know. And there's nobody there to make decisions and do the work but you. The business licences, bank accounts, insurance, issuing statements, receivables—and an entire administrative side of the business you didn't even know needed to exist—all while running flat out to make people's lives better. Thank God it was our calling or else it would have seemed a lot more like a job with negligible returns on our energy investment. We eventually got some support, found people to help with our blind spots, but something was always conspiring to hold us back from our ultimate goal: Building our very own facility.

Business growth continued on an exponential trajectory and soon we had a demand that exceeded our supply. We would have to interview, hire and on-board more people. People we *didn't* already know. And that's when things became interesting. How do you identify passion in people? How do you see their capacity to create and deliver singular experiences to clients? How do you build a culture that reflects who you are as leaders? Is this even possible?

In the early days we were the perfect combination of earnest and naïve. We just assumed that people were as passionate as us. Why wouldn't they be? And so we brought new employees on without any kind of training process. If they said they were in, then we were in! It soon became very clear that staffing was probably our number one opportunity for growth. But at the time, it was actually about to become our number one source of pain.

Our first reality check about staffing and culture came when one of our new hires decided to leave us because they felt they weren't valued enough. OK, to be clear, they felt they weren't being paid enough so they left and took clients with them. That really hurt. It's not an overstatement to say it felt like a betrayal. What had we done wrong? Better yet, as John G. Miller, author of *QBQ! The Question Behind the Question* poses, What could we have done better? How could something so simple, so good, so pure, end up so messy?

Let's just say there were lawyers, expenses, hurt feelings and when it was all said and done nobody really won. Nobody ever does in these types of scenarios, right? We'd lost valuable clients, we'd lost revenue, but most importantly we'd lost a friend.

This was a wake-up call, and we knew we had to change our HR process. We took this early mistake and tried to get better. We weren't perfect by any stretch; nobody is in a startup business. You're just pouring your heart and soul into things and that kind of singular focus can lead to blind spots. We took the blinders off and looked around, determined to see what we had missed. The first thing we noticed was that not everyone had the same focus, passion, drive and energy as we did. For some, the job was a stepping stone to somewhere else. For others, it was a cool place to hang out while they figured out what they *really* wanted to do with their lives. This wasn't who we wanted to end up with as employees but it's who we had been attracting by default. So we decided to create a blueprint for our ideal team member.

This person had to have a zest for life, which included passion about something important to them. They had to have perspective gained by real life experiences, and they had to have played on a team. Ideally, they also had knowledge of the human body and mechanics of movement. The reason this knowledge was not one of our deal breakers was because we realized knowledge could be taught. But the core values we were looking for couldn't be.

Our company wasn't a punch-in, punch-out kind of job. You couldn't show up and phone it in. There was nowhere to hide on the training floor. It was your stage; the hour was your performance, and we learned the hard way that this was really tough for a lot of people to handle.

We refined our hiring process but a lot of new employees still burned out and left. They couldn't handle the constant demand. And each time they left they continued to take clients with them. Now, the relationship with clients is personal, so we understood them following their trainer. But for us it was personal too. We'd built these relationships with our trainers over years and we had a reputation to uphold. We had given them the valuable training to support the clients they had taken. We brought employees in, gave them a place to showcase their skills, taught them how to connect with people and helped them with their confidence. We gave them the tools to succeed, and still, each time they left with clients. It was like a dagger to the heart.

Our company was doing well otherwise and so there was no one to feel sorry for us. Nobody cared because we were the "big guys." Everyone said, "Oh, just let them take a couple of people." It was absolutely everything our team ethos was *not*, so this was really hard for us to wrap our heads around. However, this was our new reality.

It was beginning to feel like something bigger was afoot. A change in the education of young trainers that had them leaving school with worse and worse attitudes. It was a sense of entitlement that we couldn't seem to screen against. It was as if people who graduated two days ago suddenly believed it was our responsibility to roll out the red carpet, or show them to the proverbial pot of gold. I think they thought their graduation was the finish line.

We established pipelines with our local universities and quickly determined ways to get the best people for our environment. Of every 20 resumés that came across our desk, three would make it into the orientation process, two would make it onto the training floor, and one would last past the three-month trial period. We ultimately dedicated a single person to HR to listen to the questions, and demands, of our staff and we did our best to meet them halfway. After all, our philosophy was that every relationship is 50/50 with each party bringing 100 per cent of themselves. We knew that all relationships broke down when one party believed they were bringing more than the other and so we compromised.

We eventually learned not to take these departures too personally, but the harsh reality was: It was a dog-eat-dog world, and we were covered in Milk-Bones®. We'd ask other entrepreneurs if they were experiencing the same thing and they confirmed what we suspected. This wasn't specific to our business. This was an epidemic everyone was trying to cure. There were shelves and shelves of "how to manage people" books in the bookstore, but not one sharing how to be a great employee. Did anyone care about being a great employee once they were hired?

Over the next few years, we made a few changes. We instituted a bonus system that kicked in after a year and we had an anonymous suggestion box set up for employees. But nothing seemed to make a real change in behaviour. Eventually profits went down and expenses went up—the classic tale of many businesses. As our employee struggles continued, the quality of our service declined and it was devastating. Despite being recognized nationally as Top 40 Under 40 business leaders, we could not get in front of the presumptive, entitled, misguided attitudes entering the workforce. We endured sleepless nights, legal battles, and members unfairly criticizing our management and leadership. At the end of the day, it just became too much to handle.

Twenty years after starting the best thing that ever happened to us, there was not much left. No passion for the people. No energy for arguing. No brilliant ideas. No joy. It was time to sell. We took the final three years to roll out an aggressive growth plan so we could leave the business on a high. We experienced our highest customer satisfaction and largest number of profitable franchises in those years. We had countless meetings with venture capital firms to determine the best way to leave the business in better shape than we started it. However, this last burst of financial success wasn't enough to make us stay. During this process, we fielded each new staff complaint with a smile and simply put an X on the calendar.

We had long ago sat across from a business owner who warned us about employees. He laughed when we told him what we were going to do and he said, "Just wait until you hire your first employees." Now we know what he meant.

Now let me be clear, our employees weren't all bad. Over two decades, we found lots of diamonds in the rough, but they were the exception, not the norm. People are the greatest assets *and* liabilities in most businesses. And they are the hardest aspect of business to influence or change.

Here's the disappointing thing: despite the skills and attitude gap that you are going to read about in the next few chapters, there are a lot of exceptions out there.

We still believe there are many young professionals with initiative and great attitudes, who we'll unfortunately never have the opportunity to lead or mentor in our company. There are a lot of great kids out there we will never take to the summit of Mount Kilimanjaro and show how to pay the process forward. There are thousands of deserving emerging leaders we would have shown the ropes to, had laughs with, shared adventures and beers with. Our negative experience, at the hands of an entitled majority, led us to sell our business and that is this group's loss.

Or maybe it doesn't have to be. Our primary motivation in writing this book is to reframe our negative experience and give it meaning. We want to reignite hope for the next generation of employees and leaders. We have put in our decades leading on the front lines and have the scars to show for it. But our belief is that the next generation can turn the tides, with the right information, motivation and tools. We want them to enjoy every opportunity that they earn, and lead in such a way that they are effective and don't end up as resentful as we were when leaving our business.

Nothing would give us greater satisfaction than to know that this book has contributed to closing the communication, skill and mindset gap between employees and leaders.

Life Literacies

1. There are inherent challenges in any startup businesses.
2. You're not going to be able to default or defer to someone else to navigate or manage those challenges on your behalf.
3. Human Resources is going to be your biggest gap, hence biggest opportunity to grow and scale your business.

4. All successful business is anchored in organizational alignment, a.k.a. culture, which is your vision, mission & values.

5. Your No. 1 challenge is going to be consistently living your culture. *Brené Brown cited 1/10 organizations they profiled were actually living their culture: vision, mission & values.

6. The point in time when the majority of people in your organization stop living the culture: vision, mission & values is the point in time where you need to pivot, re-calibrate or move on.

7. We sold what was a dream career because the number of people who did not want to embrace our culture outnumbered those who did.

References

1. Brown, Brené. *Dare to Lead: Brave work, Tough Conversations, Whole Hearts*. New York Random House. 2018.

2. Miller, John G. *QBQ! The Question Behind the Question*. TarcherPerigree. 2004.

Chapter Two

It's Not Your Fault, But It Is Your Problem

While we had our own ill-fated experience with employees, our evidence that these toxic attitudes existed was anecdotal. Even reassurance about the problem from entrepreneurs in our circle facing the same hurdles really amounted to hearsay. We wanted to quantify just how big, and how prevalent, this attitude and skill gap was becoming. We needed to study it on a larger scale.

During late 2019 and early 2020 we asked 68 executives, employers and business owners from North America, Australia, New Zealand and the United Kingdom, who have a team or teams of employees, three simple questions. We wanted to determine if the problem we saw looming was just our experience and opinion, or a more systemic, growing issue. Our three questions were:

1. Please list the top skills you see in new team members entering the workforce today.
2. Please list the skills you feel new team members are most lacking when entering the workforce.
3. What, in your opinion, are the most important skills for schools and training programs to teach for success in today's workforce?

Our hypothesis was validated. In fact it appeared the problem was already having a significant impact on businesses and teams around the world. As with interpreting any research, it is important to keep an open mind and avoid falling into mental stereotypes or judgements. There are clear trends observed through our research, but there are also outliers and those who buck the trends.

The New Workforce

According to our survey, the Top 10 skills entering the workforce are as follows:

Table 2.1: Top 10 Skills Entering the Workforce

Skill	Responses	% of Responses
Technology literacy/ adoption/ proficiency	26	10.88%
Social Media literacy	11	4.60%
Computer literacy	9	3.77%

Drive	8	3.35%
Desire/ ability to be part of a team	8	3.35%
Eagerness to learn	8	3.35%
Adaptable/ comfortable with change/ flexible/ agile	6	2.51%
Communication skills	6	2.51%
Theoretical knowledge/ information	5	2.09%
Online skills	5	2.09%

There were 104 different response trends from just this question, but even a quick review of the above answers points to some very clear groupings that were emerging from the data. When all responses were analyzed and grouped, the question produces six clear trends. They are shown below in Table 2.2.

Table 2.2: Top 6 Response Trends for Incoming Workforce Skills

Workplace Skill Trend	#	%
Technology/ computer/ online	63	26.36%
Drive/ ambition to initiate change/ energy	51	21.34%
Theoretical knowledge/ technical skills	45	18.83%
Team orientation/ belonging/ contribution	30	12.55%
Communication/ soft skills/ delivery	29	12.13%
Flexible/ adaptable/ innovative	22	9.21%

What these six trends said to us was that we are welcoming a new wave of talent that is computer, mobile, and social media savvy, driven to create change, and backed by technical and theoretical knowledge and skills. Their technical (computer and other) skills are cited at nearly four times the frequency as their communication skills.

Similarly, the desire to create change is referenced at nearly 2.5 times the frequency as the ability to be adaptive to change. This is not to mitigate or dilute the inherent value the new work regime is bringing to the workplace. We think it's quite the opposite. This dissemination of the data is done through an attempt to help. Any misalignment of aspiration and commitment leads to an inevitable disappointment for employees. In fact this is true for everyone. The goal of this entire book is to give more young people the ability to achieve their goals by understanding what is standing in the way and helping them to remove those barriers, thereby empowering them to achieve more.

Our three questions gave a good sense of what skills *are* entering the workforce but now we wanted to understand, from the employer's point of view, what skills *aren't* entering the workforce? This is an equally important question because these deficiencies are likely at the heart of all of the problems we'd experienced in our own business.

The New Problem

While our 68 executives and employers clearly saw potential in those entering the workforce, they also consistently pointed out competency and attitude gaps they experienced with their new recruits. Table 2.3

represents the Top 10 skill proficiencies employers are *not* seeing in new hires today.

Table 2.3: Top 10 Skill Deficiencies Entering the Workforce Today

Skill	#	%
Communication	25	9.06%
People / Social skills	12	4.35%
Work ethic	10	3.62%
Emotional intelligence	7	2.54%
Resilience	7	2.54%
Interpersonal relationships	7	2.54%
Realistic expectations/ pragmatism/ understanding or comprehending the commitment and effort required to be successful	7	2.54%
Drive to put in extra time/ effort to get to the next level/ going the extra mile	6	2.17%
Verbal communication	6	2.17%
Problem solving/ giving up very quickly	6	2.17%
Receiving or accepting constructive feedback	6	2.17%

Because four responses were all tied with six responses, the Top 11 responses are shown above (rather than 10). What may jump out right away to the astute observer is that communication skills showed up in both the top skills as well as skill deficiencies. Upon closer inspection, six respondents cited communication as a top skill, while 24 listed communication as a top skill gap in the workforce.

As many of the responses are linked, Table 2.4 demonstrates the "macro" trends employers are seeing (or perhaps more accurately *not* seeing) today.

Table 2.4: Skill Deficiency Trends

Workplace Skill Trend	#	%
Lack drive/ work ethic/ focus/ resilience/ "earn it" attitude	100	36.23%
Lack soft skills/ people skills/ emotional intelligence	67	24.28%
Poor communication	63	22.83%
Lack strategic/ critical thinking/ business acumen	43	15.58%
Poor teamwork	18	6.52%
Insufficient financial acumen	6	2.17%

These trends are alarming for our incumbent workforce for several reasons. First, there's the impression that young people today don't have a strong work ethic. Even worse, there's the perception that they don't really want to work for anything—just be handed it. All three authors spend time giving back to students and young professionals in various capacities, from lecturing at universities, to coaching youth sports, to mentoring and coaching the next wave of professionals. We're happy to report that we see a great many earnest, hard-working and eager young people. Unfortunately, according to our research and the anecdotal interviews with employers, these driven future professionals seem to be the exception, not the rule.

Can this be fixed? The short answer is yes. There's cause for great optimism amongst employers, educators and parents. Something isn't inherently flawed with this generation; they simply haven't been taught these things. Every one of these skill or competency gaps is teachable! We just need to make a commitment to help them change their patterns, and also understand that it's a disruptive process for young people. Lessons are likely to be met with skepticism or resistance because no one enjoys having their talent or potential questioned for the first time.

Hope for the Future

The third question we asked our employers and executives revolved around setting our younger generations up for success. In essence, how do we best prepare them for success? What skills and competencies should we be focusing on?

Table 2.5: Top 10 Skills Employers Suggest for the Future

Skill	#	%
Communication	16	7.17%
Emotional intelligence	9	4.04%
Resiliency	8	3.59%
Financial literacy / Fiscal responsibility	8	3.59%
Teamwork	8	3.59%
Leadership skills	8	3.59%

Interpersonal skills	7	3.14%
Critical thinking	7	3.14%
Work ethic	6	2.69%
Written communication	5	2.24%
Planning—from basics all the way to failing, i.e., what to do next	5	2.24%

As with Table 2.3, there were a few responses tied for 10th so the Top 11 responses are shown above. The correlation between the skill gaps employers are seeing and the competencies they suggest teaching is obvious. As with the other questions, when responses are grouped together (communication shows up twice just in the Top 10), the course of action is very clear.

Table 2.6 summarizes the top macro-trends in the skills and competencies employers are telling us are most important to teach to young professionals entering the workforce today.

Table 2.6: Skills of the Future Trends

Workplace Skill Trend	#	%
Emotional intelligence/ social/ soft skills	75	33.63%
Strategizing/ critical thinking	42	18.83%
Resilience/ work ethic	41	18.39%
Communication	36	16.14%
Personal and professional development	31	13.90%
Financial literacy	19	8.52%

The first and most important question we had as a result of this data is: Why aren't these skills being taught in school, or at work, if they're the most important?

The short answer is because they are refined skills that take time to acquire. They should be taught by professionals with sufficient experience and capability, if not mastery, in these areas. The problem is that there just isn't a Tony Robbins, Brené Brown, John Mattone, Simon Sinek or John Maxwell at every school. That being said, research by Richard Barrett and his colleagues shows a clear return on investment for those organizations placing emphasis on developing their people and organizational culture while they develop their bottom line. Their research is graphically represented in Figure 2.1.

Figure 2.1: Top 40 Best Companies to Work For (BCWF) vs S&P 500 Average Return

While investing in a new team member's personal and professional development takes time, the business case is obvious. Simply put, employees who have these skills will make you more money. When considering the business impact of employee turnover, employers cannot afford to ignore the skills gap in front of them. It's not too late. Adopting consistent, high-quality training that addresses the competency shortfalls outlined in our survey will help organizations rebuild their competitive talent and give their company a financial advantage. These are the organizations of the future.

It's a huge paradigm shift but it is the only sustainable path forward.

Life Literacies

1. Employers see young professionals entering the workforce as technically proficient.
2. Those same employers see the same young professionals as having much to be desired when it comes to the work ethic, soft skills, and reward orientation when it comes to work.
3. The skills of tomorrow aren't being taught in the proportion that they are needed today.
4. The good news is that the skills gaps our survey identified are teachable.
5. Organizations that balance developing their people (i.e., their culture) and their competitive advantage outperform their peers by as much as four-to-one on average.

References

1. Richard Barrett, The Values-Driven Organization: Unleashing Human Potential for Performance and Profit (London: Routledge), August 2013.

2. Young, Matt; Soh, Nelson: Peake, Stan. The Skills Gap Survey. 2020.

Chapter Three
What Are You Made Of?

Nothing endures the test of time that is not built on a solid foundation. Let's use the analogy of building a house. Every home starts with a foundation, which is literally a concrete or cement anchor on which to build the house frame. Once the immovable parts are in place, we customize our homes to suit personal preferences with fixtures, paint and furniture. Over time there will be deficiencies in these cosmetic pieces and most of them are quick fixes, or at the very least straightforward renovations. But we all know that deficiencies in the foundation, or framework, of a house are a lot more complicated to repair. This is why we need to make sure the materials in the foundation and the framework are high quality, durable and will stand the test of time. The same holds true for your personal make up.

In this chapter we are going to help you build a solid base on which to place the building blocks of who you are. Your building blocks will include: Your foundation created by your values, your framework comprised of your strengths and opportunities for growth, your network and, ultimately, your purpose.

Your Foundation

Every person's foundation starts with their core values. Core values are a set of underpinning characteristics that drive our decision making and behaviour. These values can include ingredients like integrity, honesty, hard work, legacy, commitment to excellence, and resilience. We typically inherit our core values from those modelled by our parents, grandparents, family or close friends. We will migrate towards the values that appeal to us and move away from those that don't appeal to us—this can fluctuate over our lifetime.

When we watch an interview of somebody who's achieved a high level of success being asked how they reached that pinnacle, we often hear them referencing their Mom, Dad, family or close friends for instilling and reinforcing the essential values that contributed to their success.

Do you know what your values are? Think about the things you like and respect the most about your upbringing—the qualities that are most important to you. Qualities that you like best about yourself. Qualities that you admire and respect in your family, friends and associates.

Write them down. If you don't feel the list is complete you can approach it a bit differently. Write down a few words describing someone you admire and take the necessary steps to add them to your list. For example, if you admire your uncle for always remembering to call you at 8 a.m. on your birthday, you might create a core value around consistency or dependability.

When coaching leaders on identifying their values, we like to use "always" and "never" statements. For instance, "I always tell the truth" reflects a core value of honesty or integrity (depending on the lens of the person), whereas "I would never cheat on my spouse" would infer a core value of loyalty, family, respect or integrity (or some combination).

In our coaching, we also invite them to think about their schedule. If "giving back" is a core value, one should be able to scroll their calendars and within a few weeks (if not days, assuming they are organized) see calendar events like "volunteer at the homeless shelter" or "coach little league." While we acknowledge that all parents are volunteers to a degree, if "giving back" is a core value, it compels you to do more than your base parental responsibilities.

It's important to remember that values can change at different points throughout our life. Some may stay consistent and others change based on the circumstances we're currently facing —and that's okay. You are not stuck with one set of values that cannot change. Also, take stock when you're struggling internally with undesirable behaviours and poor decisions. This is often an indication that your core values are being compromised.

Your Framework

Your theoretical framework is built on top of your foundation and is comprised of traits learned over a lifetime. These include things like your strengths and opportunities, impactful life moments, and your network, to name a few. Many of these traits are the sum of various experiences and help shape what you're made of.

Strength and opportunities. We don't call them strengths and weaknesses because weakness lends itself to a fixed mindset. Instead, we call them opportunities. Opportunities for growth and opportunities for change and development. Your strengths are simply the things that you're good at. For example, you may be a good communicator, good with your hands, or a great listener. Or you may be able to empathize with people, you may be highly intelligent or a great connector. It's important to know your strengths because these are your best assets. They are what you're known for. What people admire about you and come to you to access. Take a minute to think about some of your strengths. Write them down. If you're having trouble getting three to five strengths, ask somebody you trust what you do better than anyone else. According to Scudder, Lacroix, and Gallon in their book *Working With SDI*, strengths are chosen, and the strengths we choose (consciously or subconsciously) over time are a reflection of our values.

Your opportunities are the things that you're not yet good at. These are traits, habits and characteristics that you might want to pay a little bit more attention to in order to make yourself better. It's often harder to think about and list your opportunities than your strengths. If you're having trouble thinking of three to five opportunities, ask someone you trust to suggest areas for improvement. Now there's a lot of conversation about strengths-based leadership versus focusing on your opportunities. The argument is that by focusing on your opportunities you detract from what it is that you're good at and therefore end up wasting time struggling through things you need to get better at—it's an inefficient use of time. While that may be true, the point of identifying and writing down your strengths and opportunities here is to figure out what you're made of, so your opportunities for growth are an important part of the puzzle.

Next are the impactful moments of your life. These moments can be characterized as pivotal, aha moments when you were taken out of your comfort zone and forced to act, behave and respond differently. Examples of impactful moments range from divorce, personal trauma, high levels of success and achievement, extreme disappointment and adversity, all the way through to a moment of enlightenment. These instances can act as catalysts for developing a resilient mindset, or conversely, reinforce destructive behaviour as a coping or defense mechanism.

As we'll continue to say throughout this book, we cannot simply show up at the finish line without first understanding how to get to the start line. Take a few minutes to think about some of the most impactful moments of your life. How did they change your attitude and mindset? What effect did they have on you in the short-, medium- and long-term? As you reflect back on them now, is there anything you would do differently in how you handled or managed those situations? Have those moments impacted you positively or negatively along your personal development journey? How have they shaped who you've become?

It's one thing for somebody else to try to tell you the impact these moments might have had in your life, but it's completely different when that acknowledgement comes from you. The risk in not recognizing the effect of these impactful moments of your life is unknowingly behaving a certain way in similar circumstances as a result of something in your past. If you have a positive or negative pattern of behaviour it likely traces back to a moment of impact.

Your Network

As the saying goes, you are the sum total of your five closest friends. This means that a lot of the values, strengths and weaknesses, and attitudes of those people you keep company with can impact you. The reality is that you can't choose your family. They are who they are, and we need to accept them, warts and all. But we have greater control over the people outside of our family unit because we *choose* these people. These people include our classmates, our teammates and our workmates. We often attempt to surround ourselves with people that are exactly like us. People that think like us, act like us, have the same preferences as us. And while that is a good thing, it can also lead us into what is called a familiarity bias. Familiarity bias happens when we only seek out, listen to and believe one opinion. The danger of familiarity bias is that it doesn't expose us to different points of view. As we all know, there is not a one-size-fits-all silver-bullet solution to the troubles that ail society, therefore it is important to keep an open mind and take a lot of different perspectives into consideration before making judgments or decisions.

Our elders passed down sound advice to surround ourselves with people who take us where we want to go. With that in mind, it's important to keep the company of people who tell you what you *need* to hear, as well as those who tell you what you *want* to hear. Take some time to think about who your closest friends are.

Ask yourself: What are they made of? What are their values? What are their strengths and opportunities? Do they have the same values as you? Do they have the same interests as you? Do they have the ability to take you where you want to go? You're going to meet a lot of different people throughout your life who are going to fill a lot of different needs. Understanding the company you keep can and will become a reflection of who you are at any point in your life. You need to have the knowledge, tools and insight to follow your own compass in order to arrive at the destiny that was meant for you.

Your Purpose

If you have an abundance mindset, and believe that we are all put on this planet for a purpose, then you'll likely subscribe to the notion that discovering, nurturing and pursuing your purpose with relentless passion is essential. This is where we're going to dive into your personal vision and mission.

It is important to note the difference between a vision and a mission. As the famous speaker Simon Sinek noted, every successful growth movement must begin with, and is anchored by, the *why*. Why you do something gets at your motivation. Your personal vision is your *why* and serves as the guiding principle for *who* and *what* you want to be. If something comes across your path that doesn't align with your vision, chances are you would be better off avoiding it.

Factors in establishing a meaningful vision:

1. It must be inspiring. This is the ethos that you're going to wake up to every day in order to get yourself inspired and energized for the tasks at hand.

2. It must be realistic. It must reflect the realities of your capabilities and where you are at varying points in your life.

3. It must be encompassing but not overcomplicated. It has to say something about you without saying too much about you.

4. It must be what YOU want. Not what your parents or someone else wants for you.

An example of a meaningful personal vision may look like the following:

- Lifelong learner
- Trusted "go to"
- Curious adventurer

Take some time and think about what you want your personal vision to be. Think about what you're passionate about, what you're skilled at, what matters to you, and what kind of legacy you want to leave. Grab a pen and paper and start writing down examples of compelling personal visions. Once you've completed that task, share your vision with others and see what the responses are. Does it resonate with them for you? Are they surprised by the direction for you?

Much like your core values, your vision will change during different periods of your life based on the different demands, stressors and levels of achievement that you're experiencing. It is important to continue to take an inventory of where you're at in reality, and compare it to your vision, quarterly or annually, to determine whether it needs to change. Remember, this is part of the framework that's going to provide structure and sits on top of your values foundation. You want this to feel solid.

After your purpose / vision / why has been established, it's time to get specific on what you're going to do to support that vision. The mission is the logical next step.

Factors in establishing a purposeful mission:

1. It must reflect action. This is the activation part of who you are.
2. It must be measurable. This is the accountability to your actions that support your vision and values.
3. It must be easy to remember and repeat. If it's easy to remember and repeat, it's more likely to become habit.
4. It should be re-evaluated and changed on an annual basis. This should be based on the successes or learnings from the previous year, and the demands and realities of the upcoming year.

An example of a personal mission over the years may look like the following:

- 2021 *Work towards reaching the next level in all areas of my life*. Because at this point in time you might be stagnant on a lot of fronts and looking to achieve more.
- 2022 *Pay more attention to details*. Because this past year, you realized some things got away from you that you should have been on top of.
- 2023 *Save to start a family*. Because you've met someone who you're interested in sharing the next chapter of your life with.

A sound practice is to re-evaluate and re-establish your personal mission statement every November or December for the upcoming year, based on the realities of the previous year and the expectations or demands of the upcoming one. As your life changes you're going to have different demands, stressors and responsibilities that will require different focuses. Establishing a personal mission statement in front of those will increase the likelihood of achieving all of those things in the desired state.

Here's what's true about achievement: No plan. No purpose. No point. Without a well-defined mission you risk ebbing and flowing on pathways that may not be taking you where you want to go. Sharing your values, vision and mission with others, starting with those closest to you, is a great way of ensuring that you are supported and will be held accountable to what you're made of.

At the beginning of this chapter, we use the analogy of building a house with cement as a foundation, wood and steel as the frame, and furniture, fixtures and finishings as the personal nuance. We've taken a first step to help you understand what you're made of. Your values are your foundation, then working through your strengths and opportunities, impactful life moments and network, you create your framework, and then decorate with your personal vision and mission statement. In our personal and professional experience, this is the most critical, and often overlooked, exercise you can do in order to better understand *exactly* what you're made of.

Not knowing what you're made of will have severe ripple effects on your relationships, personally and professionally. All progress begins with you. Put another way, self-awareness is the start line to any form of effective leadership.

Life Literacies

1. Like concrete is the foundation of a house, your core values are the foundation of your personal and professional success. The more attention you invest in ensuring they are solid, the fewer problems you will have navigating life.

2. Your proverbial framework is comprised of personal strengths and areas of opportunity. These are usually inherited or learned from others and passed down. It's important to know what they are.

3. Your network matters. You are the sum total of your five closest friends, meaning your network is important. Sage advice is to surround yourself with people who take you where you want to go.

4. Your purpose is your guiding anchor. This is why you do what you do, and it can be articulated in the form of a personal vision and mission. As you navigate through life, it's advantageous to align with people and a profession that aligns with your purpose. Your personal fulfillment will increase substantially.

5. All progress begins and ends with you. While other people and circumstances can have an effect on your ultimate happiness, success is a system, and following these simple guidelines will help elevate you to where you want to be.

Self-reflection Questions

1. What are your values and how will you incorporate your values into your life?
2. What impactful moments or events in your life have stuck with you? How did they affect you then, and is there anything that you would do differently today?
3. Who are your closest friends and do they share the same values?
4. What is your purpose, what is your "why"?

References

1. Sinek, Simon. *Start With Why*. 2009. Portfolio Books.
2. Scudder, Tim. Lacroix, Debra. Gallon, Simon. *Working With SDI*. 2nd Ed. 2014. PSP Inc.

Chapter Four

What Are You Made For?

If building your personal identity and character is akin to building a house, then building your career is like building a skyscraper. The greater your career aspirations, the taller the building, and to support all of that height it's very important that you build it correctly from the start.

Just like building a house, the foundation of your career is your vision, values, mission and purpose. It's crucial to have a purpose that inspires you, that is larger than you, that feels too important to give up on.

For many of us, our purpose is very personal. Often times it comes from pain, a traumatic experience or adversity. Being taken advantage of. Struggling to learn something important. Or feeling left behind. All of these experiences can act as crucibles through which your purpose is born.

Your personal core values and your organizational core values may not necessarily be the same, but it's important that they are aligned. A person who has a core value around family, for instance, could easily get behind the organizational value of teamwork. On the other hand, an individual who embraces the core value of competition may not be the right fit in an organization that places a very high value on collaboration.

Just as your personal mission statement reflects your actions, an organizational mission describes how your team will go about enacting their inspiring purpose. Mission statements are, of course, highly subjective ,and while there may be no right or wrong way to write a mission statement, those riddled with corporate jargon and buzzwords are highly ineffectual. For example: "Through inspiration and collaboration we aspire to be innovative trailblazers providing maximum value for all shareholders in a sustainable way."

If we go back to building our skyscraper, then collectively, the vision, values, mission and purpose of an organization, or of an individual's career, serve as the foundation. If you've ever seen a skyscraper being built, you may notice the foundation stage is slow and unsexy. A huge hole is dug and then it seems as though nothing happens for a really long time. With a proper foundation in place, it finally appears to move quickly. Suddenly within a year there's a 60-storey building and you think, "How did that happen so fast? That went up overnight!"

We now know what constitutes the unseen or intangible aspects of your career, but then what are the visible elements? We see the windows, the walls and the floors of the building. For us these are the skills and competencies that create value for an organization and its stakeholders.

When we are finished construction, the grand entrance to our skyscraper has higher ceilings and a much more pleasing aesthetic than the rest of the building. Put another way, some skills are more foundational to success than others. One could argue that communication, emotional intelligence and other soft leadership skills are foundational and make up the Marquis floors. One could also argue that business development or sales are among these essential professional competencies. But there's one skill that all others rely on: communication.

Communication as a Foundational Skill

According to the philosopher Epictetus, "We have two ears and one mouth so that we can listen twice as much as we speak." If communication is the foundational skill for professional success then listening is the first lesson. And it's our belief there are three levels of listening.

First, low-quality, or Level One, listening is "listening to respond." In many cases when a low-level listener hears something, they want to respond so badly they won't even let the other person finish speaking. They interrupt to say their part.

In other cases, the listener focuses on only one point the speaker has made, so that everything they say afterwards has been missed. In their impatience to reply to the point, or story that resonated with them, a low-level listener has responded to one piece but missed the story altogether. In our coaching business, low-level listening is downright hazardous. In many cases, the problem that a client leads with is *not* the problem at all but rather a symptom. A Level One listener would miss this, quickly jumping in and solving the wrong problem. Whereas a wise coach asks more questions and finds the root of the problem.

A Level Two listener is someone who listens to understand. This may manifest itself by asking clarifying questions, once the other person has finished speaking. *If I heard you correctly Donna, you don't feel appreciated at work and you wish someone would notice all of the extra effort you put in without being asked. Did I catch your meaning?*

It's important to note any skill can be taken too far, or used too frequently, thereby diminishing its value. If you were to ask a clarifying question after everything that your friend says, they would likely end the painful interaction rather quickly. Besides asking clarifying questions, the most noticeable difference between a Level One and a Level Two listener is their focus. Level One listeners frequently focus on themselves. They are listening to respond with their stories and sometimes even waiting to one-up the speaker. A Level Two listener is focused on the speaker. They are present and listening with their entire body, ensuring they grasp the speaker's meaning.

What is listening with your whole body? Well, research out of UCLA in 2009 concluded that communication is 55 per cent body language, 38 per cent paralanguage (pitch, volume, intonation, etc.) and only seven per cent verbal. Listeners are perceptive to what we communicate far beyond our spoken word, so speaking is a more complex skill than most of us realize. We could write an entire book on body language alone! But here it's important to at least mention how critical the alignment between our spoken word and physical stance becomes. You can tell your boss that you are listening but if you roll your eyes, or stare out the window, while they are speaking, you're giving a very different impression. Level Two listeners are present and in the moment when conversing with others. As you will see, this is also true for a Level Three listener.

The trademark of a Level Three listener is someone who listens not just to understand meaning, but also to understand how they may be of service. If Level One is listening to respond and Level Two is listening to understand, then Level Three is listening to add value. This is not always strategic value. Level Three listeners most often listen with empathy. This listener may be a strategist who can add business acumen and insight to an idea. Or just be one who listens with immense care and concern and an innate desire to see the other person succeed. This type of listener may make a helpful introduction, nominate a friend for an award, or speak to their boss suggesting that another person deserves a promotion.

To put it simply, a Level One listener listens with their mouth, a Level Two listener listens with their ears and brain, and a Level Three listener listens with their soul. I'm sure we've all felt the difference!

In the end, listening trumps effective speaking because a misinformed, though talented, speaker may miss the mark with their audience. A great listener can always detect what matters to other people and bend their message accordingly.

One final, yet critical, point on communication and speaking is the strength of a powerful question. A question has far more power than a statement when it comes to engaging and inspiring a meaningful conversation. We've all been asked a question that changed the course of a conversation, right? Unfortunately, most people are more interested in talking about themselves than hearing about you.

In conversations, there are endless opportunities for anyone who chooses to ask more questions instead of just offering their opinions. This is not to say that your opinion does not matter, or is not welcome, however your opinion will be far more valued if offered amidst a back-and-forth conversation. And this kind of conversation always starts with a question, not a statement.

Because communication is involved in all aspects of business, communication skills are more like three-quarters of the building—not just the first floor!

Skills that Build on the Foundation

Now on top of the strong groundwork, we need to lay some other skills—ones that need to be properly communicated. Let's start with sales, perhaps the most misunderstood of all professional competencies. Sales is not convincing a buyer to give you their money. Sales is not manipulating someone into buying something that they do not need. Sales is not even making more sales than your competitor. In its purest form, sales is helping your customer and providing value before they even receive the product or service you provide. If this definition of sales comes as a shock, it's because of how many incompetent salespeople ruin the image for an entire profession. The best sales professionals in the world have mastered the art of asking powerful questions and Level Three listening. Then, and *only* then, positioning their product or service as the ideal answer to customer's needs. Good, competent sales is the lifeblood of any business. At its core, it's simply very skillful communication with potential customers.

Say you met with a fitness professional for advice on how to train for a triathlon, while nursing a knee injury. That fitness professional's only job at that point is to give the right advice on how to reach your goals. The most important questions for them to ask are not "What's your budget?" or "How much would you like to spend?"

The right questions should be whether or not you've already registered for a triathlon, what distance, and when (and even where, because this could affect your training if the course is extra hilly, or in a very hot, humid climate). The fitness professional's job is to give you the right recommendations, based on their subject matter expertise, for you to reach your goals safely. It's not about how many fitness training or physiotherapy sessions they can sell you—it's about giving you what you need.

If a client is trying to save money through the process, then the job of the fitness professional is to look at options on how you can get there safely and effectively, but also to advise you if you are taking shortcuts that could increase your risk of injury.

While safety might not pertain to other fields, the same principles apply. Recommendation-based selling is far more effective than hard-close attempts, and it all comes down to living by your values, and effective communication.

After sales, we have leadership, which is both easy to understand and much harder to define. We would suggest that great, if not holistic leadership, boils down to consistent execution of a few solid fundamentals:

1. Having a clear, compelling purpose larger than oneself.

2. Living by a set of core values that one does not compromise.

3. Assembling a group of talented team members (ideally more talented than their leader in each discipline) who can add diversity of thought and skill to enhance the team dynamic and ensure mission success.

4. As a result of the above:
   - Setting goals for oneself, one's team, and one's organization that are clear, compelling, rel-

evant, and attainable yet challenging; in the near, intermediate, and long-term horizons.

- Generating practical and innovative strategies for the attainment of said goals as a team.

5. Through example and spoken word, creating a culture that inspires the very best of each participating team member, while understanding failure and setbacks are part of the process, thus balancing expectation with understanding.

6. Establishing clarity of expectation for each team member, department or business function in terms of deliverables, deadlines, key performance metrics, and accountability.

7. Inspiring teams to be their best but patiently supporting them when they are at their worst.

8. Deflecting credit when things go well, yet accepting full responsibility when things don't go according to plan.

9. Displaying emotional regulation, behavioural and emotional consistency, and impulse control, so that the team can rely on a consistent leader, especially during times of uncertainty.

10. Readily admitting one's flaws, staying humble instead of advertising one's own merit, and finding the balance between confidence and self-deprecation in order to remain effective and build and retain trust.

11. Having processes in place for regular performance (and personal) reviews, objective performance

measures, advancement criteria, and succession planning.

Of the 11 leadership fundamentals listed above, did you notice that all have something to do with effective, if not masterful, communication? We rest our case.

Finally, we have technical skills—while under-represented in this chapter, they are still essential. Someone has to invent something, then someone else has to create workable financial models for the business, while someone else harmonizes operational systems. Data entry, physical labour, measurement, deliveries, running reports, data analysis, and many other technical skills create, improve, and bring the consumable products and services companies are based upon.

This is the reason we are stressing the "soft skills" as much as we are in this chapter, because before a new smartphone is produced with a better camera and more features, a conversation between product specialists, focus groups, leadership, and accounting professionals takes place. Before anything is designed it is dreamed and discussed.

We believe strongly that project management, engineering, accounting, innovation, security, operations, and other skills can make or break a company's success. That being said, we believe the skills that show up in everything else we do are communication, leadership and sales.

The executives and business owners we asked, based on our study, agree. Even Dale Carnegie, in his 1936 book *How to Win Friends and Influence People,* concluded that nearly 85% of one's earning potential was based more on their skills with people than their technical skills.

Theory into practice: Goal Setting and Tracking Worksheet

CONSULTING

Goal Setting and Tracking Worksheet

Name _____ **Date** _____

Support and accountability circle

Name _____

Name _____

Name _____

Name _____

Name _____

Goal	Why	Measurement	Status	Date

Remember

- Set goals in all important areas of your life: business, health, relationships, experiences/ fun, financial, personal development/ learning, and giving back.
- Set SMART goals: Specific, Measurable, Attainable, Resonating/ Realistic, and Time-bound.
- Create a plan on how to achieve each goal.
- Communicate that plan with your support and accountability circle—this is where your tribe can offer help, support, suggestions, or a reminder to never quit and get back up after any setbacks!
- Review and adjust when/ where necessary. If you're training for a half-marathon and you get injured, perhaps rehabilitating the injury is the new goal. If your goal is year-over-year business growth of 20% and a disaster happens in your business—what is the new goal if your old goal has zero chance of success? Sometimes the goal doesn't need to change, but the strategy to achieve it does. Be sure to review and adjust regularly!

Life Literacies

1. It is important that your personal and professional core values align, although they may be different.
2. There are three levels of listening.
- Level 1: with your mouth.
- Level 2: with your ears.
- Level 3: with your soul.

3. Asking questions can help ignite an engaging, inspiring, and meaningful conversation.
4. A great leader must be an effective communicator.
5. The key to continuous progress and achievement is to set SMART goals that matter in every important area in your life, and create a plan for their attainment that you share with your tribe.

Self-reflection Questions

1. What type of listener are you (Level 1, 2, or 3)? What makes you a listener at that level?
2. Assess your body language when interacting with others. Are you present and focused?
3. The 11 leadership fundamentals listed in this chapter all have something to do with effective communication. Are you an effective communicator? If not, how will you improve?
4. Have you set goals in every important area of your life, or are you planning for poor life balance without even knowing it?

References

1. Carnegie, Dale. *How to Win Friends and Influence People*. 1936. Simon & Shuster.
2. Mehrabian, A. http://www.kaaj.com/psych/smorder.html 2016

Chapter Five

What Are You Making?

With a solid foundation in place for your career skyscraper, the only place to go is up! Let's think of it this way, we have our vision, values, mission and purpose in place. Now we evaluate our educational background, skill sets and experiences to determine potential types of work we can do to achieve our goals.

Once you enter the working world, building upwards can mean different things to different people. Is it getting a promotion? Getting a raise? Building a larger, more skillful team? Or maybe simply impacting people's lives in a positive way?

Regardless of your definition of success, there is one constant that stays top of mind for most individuals— money. We serve our employers, our businesses and our valued customers in the hopes that we enrich lives, but we also want to earn enough money to support our lifestyle.

It's really even simpler than that. We all count on money to support our basic needs. Food, water and shelter all require funding. The difference in how much money we think we need lies in how simply, or lavishly, we choose to live, combined with the choices we make with our money.

Money is a funny thing. At times it can bring us what feels like endless joy and happiness, but on the flip side, it can also take us to a deep, dark place of depression, stress, anxiety and fear. The point of this chapter is to help us experience the maximum amount of joy and happiness with the money we currently earn. In other words, we are stressing the importance of financial literacy, not necessarily telling you how to make more money.

Based on our survey results, financial literacy appeared in the Top 5 skills that employers suggest employees need for the future. In addition to financial literacy being a knowledge cornerstone for our personal lives, employers are saying that literacy with money is a skill they want employees to already have when they walk through the door—regardless of the type of job they're doing.

Earlier in this book we shared the experience of heartbreak, and even betrayal, we felt from team members leaving our business for higher pay but not necessarily a better job. What people fail to realize is that earning more money is only half of the equation. In order to get the life you want, with things you want in it, you need to figure out how to achieve your financial goals. Just earning more money without a plan will likely get you nowhere.

Ask yourself these questions to spark some interesting thoughts and insights:

- When you get a new job, do you go out and reward yourself with an expensive material item or a fancy meal because you can now "afford it"?
- Do your spending habits increase as your income increases?
- When was the last time you increased how much money you save per month?
- What is the first thing you do when you receive a sum of money (holiday money, paycheque, bonus, etc.)?

The financial literacy that employers want starts at home. Your understanding and mastery of your personal finances increases your happiness and fulfilment *and* makes you a more desirable employee.

The ultimate reward of this competency is that your personal mission, vision, values and goals are supported so you can focus on building your professional life without distraction, or stress, from money concerns. With this piece solidly in place, we believe progression up the corporate ladder, or your career skyscraper, is almost limitless.

Money Talk 101

The term financial literacy can mean a whole array of things, depending on your perspective. On a personal level, we define financial literacy as the understanding of money and how money moves within our day-to-day lives. Simply put, this is the understanding of how the money we earn comes into our lives and how the money we spend goes out of our lives.

When people seek out a new job, a raise or a promotion with the primary objective to earn more money, oftentimes it's not really about the money but about the lack of understanding and control over money. People want to feel like they're in the driver's seat and they think that more money will give them that feeling. We think they are solving the wrong problem.

Our fixed expenses like rent, mortgage payments and car payments generally do not fluctuate significantly from month to month. Our variable expenses, however, like eating out, entertainment and shopping do go up and down. When we think about *needing* a raise or *needing* more money to sustain our current lifestyle, we should ask ourselves why? Maybe the need for an increase in income is primarily to pay for a bigger home or a new car.

Once you clearly identify the reason, or reasons, you need an increase, we challenge you to go a step further and dig deeper to the root of the perceived problem. Why do you need a bigger home? Are you expanding your family? Why do you need a new car? Is your current vehicle on its last legs? The answers may be yes. And then you will need an increase in income to sustain your lifestyle.

But if you realize the reason you need a raise is because your credit cards are maxed out and you want to buy the latest cellphone on the market, then you have bigger problems. Problems that, quite frankly, more money won't help you solve.

There are an infinite number of reasons why financial literacy is important, but we have narrowed it down to one basic concept—understanding the difference between a survivor versus a thriver.

Survivors live life on the edge. On a monthly basis they find that every dollar earned is spent, nothing is saved and they struggle to make ends meet. Because there is no money left at the end of the month, this group has few, if any, financial goals and no real vision for the future. This is often called living paycheque to paycheque and it's harmful to your future.

Thrivers, on the other hand, are people who are able to save money on a monthly basis. They have a clear understanding of money earned and money spent, and every financial decision they make is strategic and well thought out. Thrivers have financial goals and a plan. They live their day-to-day lives with purpose, and they have a clear vision of how their daily choices add up to their desired future.

Take a few minutes to clearly identify if you are a survivor or a thriver. If you are having difficulty determining which you are, ask yourself the following questions and answer them honestly:

1. Do I earn more than I spend each month?
2. Do I have any savings or an emergency fund?

3. Are the financial decisions that I make on a daily, weekly and monthly basis having a positive impact on my financial situation or a negative one?

4. Do I have financial goals? If so, what are my financial goals for the next year, three years, five years?

If your answer was no to all four of the questions above, at this time you are likely a survivor. Although that may seem like a bad thing, it's actually a great thing because now you have gained the awareness that you need to make changes in your financial habits.

More Money, More Problems

More money only causes more problems when we don't understand money and how to control it. Have you ever seen a friend, family member or colleague show up in a shiny new car as the result of a recent promotion, bonus, or raise?

"I earned it!" is often the refrain. Yes, you did earn it, but can you afford it? And do you need it? This is what they should be asking themselves. One of the biggest pitfalls many people face is when they earn more money, they spend more money. This is called lifestyle creep. Earn more money, spend more money, but save the same (or less). It's simple to see that it's a losing equation.

Even though they are actually earning more, their increased spending cancels it out. The formula is not actually more money = more problems, it's "more money + *more spending* = more problems."

That's not to say that we should not reward ourselves with nice new things. The purpose of financial literacy is to help us understand that getting a raise provides us with the perfect opportunity to achieve our financial goals. Things like buying a new car, new clothes or even that shiny new phone. Once we understand money and we can control it, the formula will become more money = fewer problems. Increased income in conjunction with a plan gets us to the finish line faster.

We also often hear, "I work hard, I deserve more money." There's no doubt that we all work hard, but demanding more money because of our hard work is shortsighted and even a bit entitled. In a society that is veering more and more towards instant gratification, we are losing sight of the work first, get rewarded later attitude. We want it all now. We encourage people to change their mindset and instead of focusing on money that should be coming into your life, take a closer look at the money going out of your life. One of the best ways to save more money is to spend less. Simple, right?

People who go into work every day to essentially wait for the next pay day are putting themselves on an unnecessary rollercoaster of emotions. Think about it. They wait for pay day and then live the next few days happily spending most, if not all, of their paycheque. After that, they spend the next week or two depressed, stressed and full of anxiety because they don't have any money to spend or cover expenses. And likely their credit cards are maxed out with compound interest growing at an astronomical rate.

It's a terrible ride. Taking you to the heights of happiness and then, just as quickly, bringing you down to the depths of despair.

Save yourself from this nightmare and take some time to think about where you spend your money and how you spend it. Are there areas in your life where you can cut expenses? Do you need these things or do you want them?

We all know there's a difference between a need and a want but most people still confuse the two. Needs are things that we must have in order to survive. Food. Shelter. Water. Wants are things that add comfort to our lives. Getting a new car to replace a perfectly good old one. Buying a new cellphone to replace one that still works.

That's not to say that we should get nothing we want, but many people need to take a long hard look at their financial landscape and start making choices that align with their vison of the future and not just their moment-to-moment desires.

Think of personal financial literacy as the bridge between where we are and where we want to go. When we have mastery over our financial life we can allocate our time and efforts to other important things like building our figurative skyscrapers.

Money has Super Powers

Now you're onboard and making better choices but I know many of you are still thinking, "How can I make more money?" It's a good question and one that stumps most people.

The most common approach to making more money is to work more hours or to get another job (and therefore work more hours). Here's a thought, what if we could let our money work *for us*? After all, there are only 24 hours in a day and we can't possibly work all 24 hours to earn money, right?

Financially literate people often have a plan and part of that plan often involves what they do with the money that they've saved up. Most of us know we should be investing our money. But this means many different things to different people. Everybody invests in different ways.

One commonality amongst all investors, and investments, is that you use money to make more money. We aren't going to get into the details of what types of investments are out there, or give you advice on how to invest your money. There are experts that dedicate their careers to analyzing the market and advising people on investment options based on their desired outcomes and goals.

What we will share with you is the concept of compound interest and how this can change your financial well-being.

When you invest your money, you hope to earn interest, which is income on your investment. Compound interest is the interest that you earn *on top* of the interest you already earned. It may sound confusing, so let's break it down.

SCENARIO 1:

You have exactly $1,000 to invest today and you will not be making any other contributions to the investment in the upcoming months or years. You decide to invest your money with hopes to earn a conservative five per cent annual return.

In the real world, money faces inflation. More money gets printed every year and thus the value of money is actually declining over time. To stay focused on the fundamental principles, we will not consider inflation when presenting these scenarios.

In exactly one year from the investment date, you earn five per cent interest.

$1,000 x 5% = $50 interest earned. New total = $1,050.

Let's say you keep the new total of $1,050 in the investment for another year and it earns another five per cent interest.

In year two, you will not earn $50 in interest; you will earn $52.50 because you are now earning interest on $1,050, not $1,000. This is $2.50 more than in year one because you earned interest on the interest earned in year one (the $50). This is called compound interest.

If we continue this example over 10 years, our initial investment of $1,000 with five per cent compound interest will have a total value of $1,629. That amounts to a total of $629 of interest earned by letting your money work for you.

Take a look at the chart below and you can see that after year one, no extra money is invested but the amount of interest earned on the initial investment grows. This is the power of compound interest and this is a great tool to help you achieve the financial goals you have set for yourself while making the most of the 24 hours in the day.

Year	Invest-ment	Annual interest (assumed 5% interest rate)	Total interest	Total value
1	1,000.00	50.00	50.00	1,050.00
2	0.00	52.50	102.50	1,102.50
3	0.00	55.13	157.63	1,157.63
4	0.00	57.88	215.51	1,215.51
5	0.00	60.78	276.28	1,276.28
6	0.00	63.81	340.10	1,340.10
7	0.00	67.00	407.10	1,407.10
8	0.00	70.36	477.46	1,477.46
9	0.00	73.87	551.33	1,551.33
10	0.00	77.57	628.89	1,628.89

SCENARIO 2:

You don't have a lump sum of cash to invest today, but you have decided to commit to a savings plan where you will contribute $50 a month into an investment portfolio (even if that means cutting the fancy lattes and dining out). You decide to invest your money with hopes of earning a conservative five per cent annual return.

One common money myth is that you have to be rich to invest. You don't have to be rich but you have to have a plan. It might not seem like a lot, but saving $50 a month over 10 years can bear some serious fruits for you.

It gets a bit more complex with monthly payments because in most cases, interest compounds monthly, meaning that at the end of the calendar year, $50 contributed in January will earn interest for 12 months, whereas $50 contributed in November will earn interest for two months.

In year one (after 12 months), with $50 contributed at the end of the month, the total amount you will have invested is $600. The monthly contributions earn interest over time and the annual interest earned is approximately $13.63.

In year two, your starting point will be $613.63, which earns compound interest. In addition to your monthly payments, at the end of year two your investment should grow to be about $1,258.

The chart below shows the annual breakdown over 10 years. We can see that the total interest earned over 10 years with consistent monthly contributions of $50 per month is $1,718. The power of compound interest and time has the potential to turn $6,000 into $7,718. The beautiful part is that we are letting our money work for us.

This scenario proves that it does not require a lot of money to invest and we do not have to have a large amount before we start investing. Start small and within your means. With time, patience, and a consistent effort, you can create wealth.

	Annual investment	Total investment	Interest earned in the year	Total interest earned	Total value
1	$600.00	$600.00	$13.63	$13.63	$613.63
2	$600.00	$1,200.00	$44.31	$57.94	$1,257.94
3	$600.00	$1,800.00	$76.53	$134.47	$1,934.47
4	$600.00	$2,400.00	$110.35	$244.82	$2,644.82
5	$600.00	$3,000.00	$145.87	$390.69	$3,390.69
6	$600.00	$3,600.00	$183.16	$573.85	$4,173.85
7	$600.00	$4,200.00	$222.32	$796.17	$4,996.17
8	$600.00	$4,800.00	$263.44	$1,059.61	$5,859.61
9	$600.00	$5,400.00	$306.61	$1,366.22	$6,766.22
10	$600.00	$6,000.00	$351.94	$1,718.16	$7,718.16

SCENARIO 3:

You're a superstar saver and you have $1,000 today to invest AND you commit to saving $50 a month for the long-term future. With all factors consistent with the scenarios 1 and 2 above, the chart below shows what the 10-year results could look like.

With this investment plan, a total investment of $7,000 (contributed over the span of 10 years), could earn a total of $2,347 in interest alone! We really meant it when we said that compound interest and time could change your financial well-being.

	Annual investment	Total investment	Interest earned in the year	Total interest earned	Total value
1	$1,600.00	$1,600.00	$63.63	$63.63	$1,663.63
2	$600.00	$2,200.00	$96.81	$160.44	$2,360.44
3	$600.00	$2,800.00	$131.65	$292.09	$3,092.09
4	$600.00	$3,400.00	$168.23	$460.32	$3,860.32
5	$600.00	$4,000.00	$206.65	$666.97	$4,666.97
6	$600.00	$4,600.00	$246.98	$913.95	$5,513.95
7	$600.00	$5,200.00	$289.33	$1,203.27	$6,403.27
8	$600.00	$5,800.00	$333.79	$1,537.06	$7,337.06
9	$600.00	$6,400.00	$380.48	$1,917.55	$8,317.55
10	$600.00	$7,000.00	$429.51	$2,347.05	$9,347.05

You may not be in a position to put a lump sum of cash into an investment account at this moment but we must remember that everything takes time. Compound interest also takes time. The three scenarios above clearly show that you do not need a lot of money to invest and that a little goes a long way (over time).

If you are in a position where you want to start to save up money to be able to start an investment, we challenge you to think about your daily, weekly and monthly expenditures and see where you can eliminate spending and put money aside. A $5 coffee purchased four times a week appears to be only $20 a week, but over one year this amounts to $1,040 ($5 x 4/week x 52 weeks/year). Eye-opening, isn't it?

A Financial Void

One of the biggest gaps that we find when talking to people about money is the lack of a personal budget. Everyone needs a budget, but most choose not to have one because they are tedious to maintain, appear to be scary, and give off a limiting vibe.

Creating a budget is one of the best things you can do for yourself financially. A budget is a plan of how you are going to spend your money. Money needs direction. As humans, we tend to spend money emotionally, so without a plan, we end up spending money on things that we don't necessarily need.

Budgets are misunderstood. They are used as a scape-goat for those that do not want to take full control and accountability of their personal finances and financial literacy.

Most people who operate without a budget have no clue where their money goes each month. We've all heard (and some of us have said it), "I don't want to see what my credit card bill looks like." This is one of the most financially harmful sayings and situations that you can put yourself in.

The real truth about budgets is as follows:

1. They are not tedious if they are created effectively and maintained frequently.
2. They are not scary if they are kept as simple and easy to read as possible.

3. Budgets do not always create limitations. They actually enable you to spend on things that you want as long as funds are allocated appropriately.

Budgets can be a great tool to help you take control of your financial situation if they are used properly and consistently.

Filling the Void

Budgets do not have to be complex. Most people envision a budget to be a giant spreadsheet with numbers and formulae present everywhere. Just thinking about such a complex system is scary, even to us.

Most people create budgets at the beginning of the month and review it once a week to ensure they are on track. Reviewing your budget once a week will help you stay on track with your spending and goals. This may seem like a daunting task, but if your budget is simple and easy to pick up, it doesn't take much time.

Generally, a budget will include the following sections:

1. Income: A complete list of all your sources of income.
2. Savings: How much do you plan to save for your future or your emergency fund?
3. Fixed expenses: Expenses that have a set dollar amount each month. Usually fixed expenses are needs that include things like rent, phone bill, and car payments.

4. Variable expenses: Expenses that vary month over month. These are the ones that we must watch closely because they are most likely to go over-budget. Examples of variable expenses include dining out and entertainment.

5. Goals: How much money will you allocate towards your financial goals?

6. Remaining cash: How much cash is left at the end of the month after factoring in your savings, expenses and goals? If the amount is negative, you must revise your allocation because this means you are spending more than you earn.

An effective budget format can look something like this:

INCOME	EXPECTED	ACTUAL

SAVINGS	BUDGET	ACTUAL

EXPENSES	BUDGET	ACTUAL

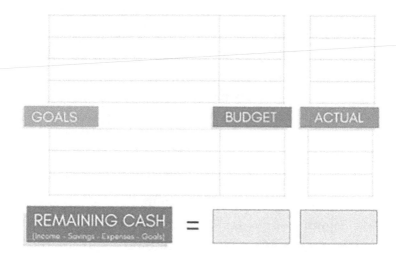

In each section, there are two columns. The first column ("expected" and "actual") are used when you are planning your budget at the beginning of the month. The "actual" column is used to record how much you spent in each category as the month progresses.

At the end of the month, it's best to review your expected income and budgeted expenses versus what you actually earned and spent. Once you have a budget in place, you will be more conscious of where your money goes and your financial literacy will level up.

Life Literacies

1. Earning more money with poor financial literacy will leave you in the same place you started. More money is only part of the solution. We must know how to manage the money once we earn it.

2. Survivors consistently live paycheque-to-paycheque by choice. Thrivers choose financial literacy, which allows them to create wealth and achieve their financial goals. Which one are you today? And which one would you like to be?

3. More money + more spending = more problems. Learning the difference between needs and wants will change your financial situation.

4. Don't underestimate the power of compound interest and don't sell your future-self short by thinking that you have to be rich to invest. You can start with almost nothing, but it takes consistency, a plan and patience to be successful.

5. Creating a budget is one of the best things you can do for yourself financially. Everyone needs a budget to stay on track—stop making excuses about why you don't need one!

Self-reflection Questions

1. What actions will you take to improve your current financial situation?

2. How will you create, adjust or enhance your personal budget?

3. What are your financial goals and what is your action plan to achieve them?

Chapter Six

What Are You Becoming?

"We are what we repeatedly do. Excellence, then,
is not an act but a habit"
—Will Durant (paraphrasing Aristotle)

I f we subscribe to the belief that success is a system, then one of the most important practices we should work to implement in our day-to-day lives is routine. Having a solid routine, or more accurately, a set of routines, helps us stay on track and focused in an increasingly distracted world. Some may go as far as to suggest that routines are the foundations of healthy personal and professional habits. Again, no plan, no purpose, no point. Many successful people will attest to the reality that where there is no routine, there's chaos.

The first routine we should look to solidify is our morning one. Are we waking up to click on our devices and becoming ensnared in the irrelevant news trap? Or are we priming our physical and mental state to attack the day? Do we wake up on purpose, or hit snooze five times? The goal of a morning routine is to engineer the best physical and mental state possible, so that we can increase the likelihood of having the best day possible.

Our acronym for a GREAT day is as follows:

- **G**ratitude. Begin your day by placing yourself in an immense state of gratitude for all that is good in your life. It might be your parents, friends, dog, job, significant other, even the weather forecast that day. If some area of your life is bothering you, move past it for this part of the routine.

- **R**elationships. Reflect on the state of all of the important relationships in your life. This can include, but is not limited to: parents, siblings, extended family, friends, significant other, any important business or spiritual relationships—and don't forget your relationship with yourself! Self-care is a critical component of sustained success.

- **E**xercise. Move your body every day. It doesn't have to be a crazy intense fitness class or a 10-mile run. It could be push-ups, walking, stretching, yoga, Tai Chi, or your rehabilitation routine from your physiotherapist if you're nursing an injury. Our physical state has a major influence on our mental state, and challenging exercises help build our resiliency muscle—so move your body every day (in a safe and reasonable manner appropriate to your fitness level).

- **Achieved.** Picture all of your tasks for the upcoming day. Picture your math exam, or the job interview, or the sales meeting with Greg, all going 100 per cent according to plan, a smashing success! Visualize what success looks like, and try to reverse-engineer what it will take to drive each of your important tasks to your desired outcome.

- **Tweak.** Keeping the above desired outcomes in place, do you have 20 monumental tasks on your plate for today? Is it realistic they will all be home runs? Do you have two tasks on your plate, and might you be "sand-bagging" your bar for success? Tweak your day accordingly (professionally, we don't advocate cancelling meetings last-minute just because you're busy).

All we're ever guaranteed is today; the one day in front of us that we are living right now. The secret to creating the best life possible (and therefore those who we spend the most time with) is to make each day the best it can be—one day at a time.

The second routine we should look to master is our transition from home to work. Are we driving, using public transit, or carpooling? Is there traffic? There are things we can, and should, consider on our way to work in order to frame the day for success. This is especially important when starting a new job. Did you budget enough time for traffic to get to work on time? Do you know the public transit peak times, or are you just assuming there will be room on the bus or subway for you when you show up? If we have a big day ahead, it might also be important to consider clearing our minds, listening to music or tuning into our favourite talk radio show so as to enter the workplace in an ideal state of mind. Most people drive to work on "autopilot," not considering how the idle chatter of the radio deejays, or the type of music they are listening to, might be affecting their energy and emotional state. Success doesn't happen on autopilot, and it's not an accident—decide to be better in every aspect of your day!

When we arrive at work, we should have a work-arrival routine so we can make sure we're setting ourselves up on the front end of the work day as proactively as we can, instead of as reactively as possible. Five tips for this include:

1. No distractions. Don't have 12 browsers open at once, and don't have your phone staring at you while you're trying to type while listening to music while eating if it's a task requiring focus.

2. Set yourself up for success by planning. For instance, if the first task you try to accomplish in your day is creating a slide deck for an important meeting, and your time estimate is two hours, then don't start when you get to your desk if there's a morning meeting starting in 15 minutes. Budget your day into chunks of time, and allocate the ap-

propriate activities into time slots that make sense around your important meetings and other scheduled events.

3. First things first. Your to-do list should be prioritized. If not, your first priority is to prioritize your to-do list. Once done, begin the day with the important stuff and get to the "nice to do" stuff when it's nice to do. Tackle the "need to do" items when you need to do them—which is always first.

4. Move throughout the day. Our ancestors were hunters and gatherers. Do you think we were born to sit for nine-plus hours a day? Change your seated position every half hour, and every 90 minutes, get up to drink water, use the washroom, or even take a short walk and change your surroundings.

5. Fuel the machine. Drink plenty of water and limit excess caffeine intake. Eat healthy foods and do not wait until you're starving to eat lunch. The hungrier you get, the less you care about nutrition, and the faster and more you eat. This is a dangerous combination, which is why some young professionals can gain up to 20 pounds or even more during their first year in an office setting if they are used to being more active and not intentional about fueling their body. Furthermore, junk in = junk out. You don't put regular unleaded fuel in a Formula One race car. Similarly, you can't sustain high levels of focus and performance on chips, candy bars and other junk food or processed foods.

The same goes for the work day. Research reported in the *Harvard Business Review* showed that the average employee gets interrupted 50 to 60 times per day, and around 80 per cent of these interruptions aren't important. Having a solid routine of when you are going to take breaks, check your social media, and deal with personal issues and other things will not only increase your efficiency but decrease your stress as others learn when they can and should engage you during your workday (and when they shouldn't).

Your end-of-the-day routine is just as important as your beginning-of-the-day routine. Work is done and if you have pets, children or significant others, this is when your proverbial second jobs will commence. The negative stresses start to appear when we don't turn our time or attention off of work and onto other important facets of our lives. This work-life balance is discussed in detail in Stephen Covey's *The 7 Habits of Highly Effective People* where he breaks into great detail the power of habits, with routine being one of them. Five tips for a successful end-of-the-day routine may include:

1. Everything has a place. Instead of throwing your keys in some random place, your jacket some other place it doesn't belong and your wallet wherever you happen to be, find a tidy, consistent, singular place for each of these items. This saves time later and prevents making you late because you had to look for these items.

2. The 100 per cent rule. When you're at work—focus on work, not the upcoming weekend or basketball

game on TV that night. When you're at home—be home. When you're with your friends—be with your friends, not having your face five inches from your phone screen. If you can't focus at home because you've got that major project that isn't finished, get it done right away, otherwise you aren't enjoying your time with family or friends because you're preoccupied with an unfinished task at work.

3. Plan your life, not just your work. Dinner with friends, your spin class, anything else that's important to you should make its way onto your calendar. If you show us someone who only uses their calendar for work, we'll show you someone who complains at least some of the time about life balance.

4. Sharpen the axe (in all areas of life). While we all have long days that leave us craving the couch the moment we walk in the door, we shouldn't "turn off" completely at home. Learning is an essential skill for life—all of life. You might be reading a book about sales to grow in your career, but what about relationships? Finance and investing? Parenting? Mindset? Fitness and nutrition? Even learning a new language or new skill helps us to sharpen the axe, so to speak. One of our author's sons taught him how to play chess at the age of 43 just this past year!

5. Set yourself up for success the night before. Set out tomorrow's clothes (workout and school or work) the night before. One less decision to waste cognitive function or time on when you're tired (former President Obama had his staff lay out two outfits every day, limiting his choices and conserving his cognitive function for the big decisions).

The last routine we recommend is a nightly review. Reflecting on how you did each day compared to your goal is a great way to learn, move unaccomplished tasks to the next day and, over time, improve the accuracy of what you're able to accomplish in a day. It may take 15 or 20 minutes the first few times you do this, and that may feel like you're "working in your free time," but eventually this will cut down to five to 10 minutes, and will help you get a lot more done, and get a lot more satisfaction, out of tomorrow's eight hours. Furthermore, any millionaires we've ever worked with—the level of success that most people are envious of—"worked for free" at first to hone their craft and ultimately achieve that level of success.

There is no question that having a solid, consistent routine can help keep you on track, focused and on-point, and more importantly it will alleviate stresses associated with feeling unorganized, unprepared and uninformed. In creating a routine, think about starting small and focus on the positive, repetitive tasks you can accomplish. It's great to establish a routine when you're just starting out and don't have all of the responsibilities of a full-blown working professional who's also overseeing a family, because you will be well practiced to add, adjust and delegate as you need.

Start small, with what you have, now. Great routines improve over time when they are applied consistently and with discipline. As Zig Ziglar famously said, "You don't have to be great to start, but you have to start to be great."

Life Literacies

1. A very large portion of our life boils down to repetitive behaviours. These behaviours can be understood, changed and optimized.
2. The creation of and adherence to effective routines increases the likelihood of producing desired outcomes—for instance, having a G.R.E.A.T. day.
3. When we maximize one day at a time, we maximize our lives, including who and what we become.

Self-reflection Questions

1. How will you make every day a G.R.E.A.T. day?
2. What is your work-arrival-routine? If you don't have one yet, take some time to create one.
3. What is your daily routine from start to finish? What will you do to ensure you stay consistent in your routine?

Resources

1. https://hbr.org/2019/12/10-quick-tips-for-avoiding-distractions-at-work

2. Covey, Stephen. The 7 Habits of Highly Effective People. 1989. Free Press.

Chapter Seven

The Four Stages of an Employee's Journey

You've received your diploma or degree, your "welcome to the team" package, and are now officially ready to go. The first day at your new career is filled with so many emotions it can be difficult to anticipate what's coming next. Or is it?

What would you give to know exactly what you can expect throughout your employment journey? Would it help you be better prepared? Would it alleviate your anxiety and stress? Would it help you better navigate one of the longest and most important journeys in your life? The fact is, despite row upon row of literature and endless Google searches on how to be a great manager or owner-operator, advice on how to be a great employee is virtually non-existent—until now.

With more than two decades of working with employees, we would have given a lot to understand the ins and outs and ups and downs of the employee journey, specifically from the perspective of professional development. It was through this lens, and the experience of helping over 250 small, medium and large businesses identify their employee growth opportunities that we've identified the four stages employees must pass through en route to becoming truly irreplaceable business assets.

Let's begin the employee's journey.

The New Hire

Let's face it, there are few things in life more exciting than starting your new career. It's like a first date and you are more than keen to put your best foot forward. You arrive early, listen intently and laugh at office jokes you don't find remotely funny, all in attempt to fit in. You know damn well you will be evaluated, and likely judged, by the veteran teammates and management on everything from how you look and act to your knowledge and job skills.

You accept that you're likely to be talked about for a three-month minimum, barring some catastrophic mistake. You listen intently and take it all in because you know the name of the new-hire game is to learn fast while making as few mistakes as possible. And you're likely more than willing to pitch in and go the extra mile because that's going to make you more likable and more valuable faster.

Over decades of leading and mentoring new hires, we've shared 10 helpful tips to put your best new-hire foot forward:

1. Do your homework. It's to your advantage to do as much homework as you can prior to crossing the threshold on day one. If you've already landed the opportunity, you likely know the company vision, purpose, mission and values, and determined your alignment. If not, it's still not too late. These are not a billboard advertisement. They are intended to be lived daily. Understand what they are.

2. How to put your best foot forward 101. Arrive early and stay late. This is the easiest habit to show the type of person you are. If the workday begins at 9 a.m., that means you are in the office, at your desk, with your coffee, cleared conversations and beginning work at 9 a.m. With respect to completing tasks, you should work to complete the goals for the day instead of ending your work day based on the clock.

3. Listen intently and take notes. Every new hire needs to listen intently and take notes. With each new job comes a steep learning curve and the biggest turnoff for employers has to be telling new recruits the same thing multiple times. Taking notes and reflecting on them at the end of the day is also a great way to recall and build upon what you've heard and learned.

4. Ask questions and seek clarity. The only bad questions are the ones you have not asked or the ones you've already been told. You are the new hire, not the new hero, and everyone who has come before you has gone through the same learning process at some point in their career.

5. Be comfortable with being uncomfortable. The work environment is fluid and you may be called on to do things you're not quite familiar with, that fall outside of your perceived skill set, or that you've tried and failed to execute. This is where the real learning happens. The saying "you're either winning or you're learning" is very apt and the sooner you can embrace this, the more successful you're going to be.

6. Get to know your teammates. Make the time to research and introduce yourself to your co-workers, the management team, and ownership. Learn about their work experience, habits, hobbies, and likes and dislikes in their role, and use that knowledge to create meaningful conversation and connection.

7. Stay office neutral. Where possible, avoid being recruited into a clique or attached to a group. You want to be able to form and make your own decisions based on your own impressions, independent of the influence of others. Avoid office politics whenever possible.

8. Work in the moment. Be "all in" to master the responsibility at hand. Avoid comparing past work environments and accomplishments. Try not to think too much about what your next career move is before mastering your current role.

9. Have a 30-60-90-day plan. This is a personal and professional plan that can help keep you on track and avoid being overwhelmed with the day-to-day requirements. Planning helps create positive daily habits, so you are in front of your responsibilities instead of being consistently stressed out trying to play catch-up.

10. Never forget how you started. You wouldn't be ok if your employer paid you $50 per hour to start, then paid you gradually less each week. The reverse is also true. The reality is that to become an organizational asset (meaning you are helping the organization generate efficiency, purpose and income), you should be constantly seeking to improve your contribution each week with the same level of enthusiasm you started with. This is difficult because people forget where and how they started.

Keep these 10 steps in mind. Executing them consistently is what's going to help you learn fast while making as few mistakes as possible. You can expect this stage to last a minimum of 90 days to a year and, upon mastery, you'll progress from new hire to the next stage of your journey: the performing teammate.

The Performing Teammate

Congratulations, you've progressed onto the next stage of your employee journey: the performing teammate. Fitting in nicely, you've demonstrated the ability to learn information and implement tasks and process with above-average efficiency. And wouldn't you know it, there's someone else wearing the new hire label after you!

As a performing teammate, you execute your job description and uphold minimum company standards and culture. You're in a rhythm, getting comfortable and gaining confidence. This confidence is helping others around you rely on you to complete tasks. And don't forget what got you to this stage of your journey! It's well known that the kiss of death for any achiever is complacency.

Three top characteristics of a performing teammate include:

1. Reliability: Assigned tasks are completed on time, on budget and up to the standard.
2. Dependability: When someone needs something, the performing teammate can be counted on to deliver.
3. Accountability: The performing teammate never fails to deliver on what they said they would do and when they said they would do it.

One of the biggest misnomers of performing teammates is feeling the need or pressure to *have to* move to the next stage—high performer. This isn't true. There is tremendous value in quality people doing quality work on a consistent basis. In fact, most organizational growth depends on it. The performing teammate stage can last from post-new-hire stage through one to five years or even the entire duration of a career.

Having said that, we know there are internal and external pressures to climb the corporate ladder or reach that next pay grade—and that's usually where things start to go sideways. The new hire and performing teammate stages of the employee journey are predominantly focused on managing oneself, and while not easy, they are significantly easier and different than having to manage additional processes and other people. Too many times, we see people aspiring to fast-track to the high-performing teammate stage of employment, taking on responsibilities they are not yet prepared, well-suited or wired for, which creates dysfunction.

Five considerations of every performing teammate prior to accepting additional responsibility are:

1. Am I happy with the role I'm in and the level I'm at? If yes, then what is the impetus for change?
2. Have I mastered the role I'm in and stage I'm at? If no, then what else can I and should I be learning?
3. What new skills will I have to learn in order to continue to the next stage of my employee journey? How will I schedule time to learn those while continuing to consistently implement?
4. What is the return on investment in progressing to the next stage? Is that return aligned with my personal skill set and professional goals?

5. Are my personal life goals aligned with my professional life goals if I take on more responsibility? If not, then be patient until they are.

Even with an increasingly transient workforce trying on new jobs with a much higher frequency than former generations, we need to remember that professional development is a marathon, not a sprint. Book smarts and online courses are no match for the experience gleaned through real-time doing, and like it or not, no matter where you go, there you are.

If you have determined your time in the performing teammate stage has served you well and you're seeking your next professional challenge, you'll enjoy the excitement as you transition from managing your day-to-day to stepping up as a high potential.

The High Potential

By now, you've demonstrated that you're a great example of living the values of the organization. You can be pointed to as an example of those who embody the organizational culture and the ideals the team standards are.

By proving yourself time and time again through being organized, taking initiative, working hard and demonstrating a great attitude, you've gotten noticed. What you may not know is that your manager meets with their peers at least twice a year to discuss the "up-and-comers" within the organization and your name has just been placed on the list. What's important to know about "the list" is that it's not written on a stone tablet. Your name can come off just as quickly as it appeared.

While your past behaviour has earned you a place at the table, what you need to know is that as a high potential, more will be expected in terms of your future behaviour. The values, vision, mission and purpose of the organization are there to inspire what could be; and you're now counted on to be a living example of all of these concepts for your coworkers.

Unbeknownst to you, conversations that you weren't even a part of have changed your trajectory, and also the filter through which your performance is measured. When you stepped up in the past, it was called "going over and above." Now, it's expected behaviour. When you met all of your deliverables before, it was a "job well done." If leaders across the organization who just heard your manager advocate for you don't see you step up, they might actually argue against your inclusion. The standards have changed and it's very possible that no one thought to tell you.

The other possible surprise for high potentials is that the tests thrown at them are going to change. If you think back to your onboarding, everything was laid out in a sequential, step-by-step fashion that made it easy for you to see a roadmap to your future development and success.

As a veteran with the company, and one of its brightest stars, you're now entering a place of contribution within the organization which is fluid, and does not have a set-in-stone road map. Great companies look to hire and promote from within—and the best way of getting internal candidates ready for new jobs is to challenge them. In other words, it may feel like you were being shown how to build your career brick-by-brick and now it might feel like the bricks are being thrown to you (or at you) from all angles.

It is important to remember, as you inevitably find yourself outside of your comfort zone, the fundamentals that got you here. By this we mean the habits, attitudes and disciplines that made you successful, not just your strengths and skills. If your manager is doing their job, they will be challenging you to grow your capability, as Marshall Goldsmith eloquently put it, "What got you here won't get you there."

Lastly, don't forget to communicate if you are being pushed too hard, too fast, or in ways that you feel are more likely to break you down than build you up. If you communicate proactively and respectfully, any good leader will be more than happy to meet you halfway and tailor their approach.

Four important keys for the high potential to remember are as follows:

1. Great companies look to grow from within by promoting people they can trust.

2. Greater challenges and more responsibility are some of the greatest compliments a team member can receive—it means you have a bright future!

3. If it feels like the goal posts have been moved in terms of your performance, don't take it personally and try not to react emotionally. It's probably a

good (if not great) sign that your manager is busier than you are. This is not an excuse for poor communication but this is a reality of the workplace.

4. When your name gets presented as a high potential, more people within the organization will be watching you more closely than your manager. Even though it feels like you already have, it's time to step up your game or, at bare minimum, maintain the same standard that got you noticed in the first place.

Keep these points in mind and you're well on your way to winning big. When you win, the team wins, and when you win at the fourth stage of your employee journey, the team wins in bigger ways than ever before.

The Role Player

When you have taken every challenge thrown at you and found ways to learn and grow through the process, it's time for you to start to influence the process. When you have shown high competency and high character throughout the entry level journey to start your career, then you have earned a post as a role player. This is a team member with increased responsibility who is more directly responsible for setting the team and organization up for success through their contribution.

You might be asked to lead a small team, department, or business function. Ultimately, the skills that you will be evaluated on have changed. All of the pre-requisites that got you here in terms of your attitude, work ethic, values and team dynamic will still be required as a bare minimum for any teammate. However, now you're likely to also be measured on deadlines, budgets and possibly even the performance of other people.

You have a lot more responsibility *and* a lot more opportunity to influence change that will have an impact in your success and the success of others. You might feel like you're under a microscope, like there's nowhere to hide, but it means people know that what you do matters—that the bus slows down if you're not on it.

One of the greatest sources of stress we can have is to feel hopeless and powerless to affect our own outcomes. To feel that we are merely pawns in the game and that the game and our fate are decided by others. At the level of role player, there may be more responsibility and more pressure, and in a sense there is more freedom because you can see how influencing the variables within your control creates a better situation and more opportunity for you and others.

Just like the high-potential stage, expectations of your performance and your behaviour have changed. This time, you might not be surprised—you might have a whole new job description and you might even be reporting to a new manager because of your promotion or transfer.

You might find yourself with parts of your job that you feel unprepared for. You might be a skilled marketing professional and now you find yourself as a client relationship lead or managing budgets for the digital marketing department. It might be new territory, perhaps like never before, but the "powers that be" have put you in the position because they believe you'll be able to make the adjustments and learn on the job. For these reasons, the last thing you can do is to stop learning.

Learning happens in many forms. Besides learning on the job, take the initiative to shore up any areas you might be struggling with—here are five possible learning methods:

1. Listen to a podcast focused on the areas you're trying to learn more about.

2. Take a course; whether through a university (even if online) or through online course providers like Udemy.

3. Take a book on the road (or anywhere else). Audiobooks are becoming more popular and more accessible every day.

4. Join a mastermind group. There are learning and professional development groups for almost everything today. Meetup groups, professional associations, and online groups on Facebook and LinkedIn are all great alternatives if you can't find or afford a mastermind group.

5. Seek out a mentor (or mentors) in the areas that you hope to improve. Mentors can be found in your company or elsewhere in your industry. With online content growing by the second, you might find a mentor you never even meet by consum-

ing their content on LinkedIn, YouTube and other platforms.

Regardless of your new role and how skilled you are at this moment, chances are you're going to have to improve in the following critical skills to be successful as a role player and beyond in your career:

1. Time management, organization and prioritization: We all have the same 24 hours in a day and the best of the best know how to use the time they have to get more done.

2. Communication: Effective listening and speaking go a long way to achieving buy-in from others, having your ideas accepted and even achieving more sales.

3. Persuasion: By persuasion we mean being able to influence. In no way do we mean manipulation. Persuasion is an important skill in conflict resolution, leadership, sales and marketing, and even getting the team to implement better safety practices.

These skills in particular are transferrable, meaning they apply to a great many types of jobs in a great many industries. So many professionals we've worked with "pigeonhole" themselves by their job title. A prep cook, for instance, who works their way to line cook and then decides to leave the restaurant industry doesn't do so empty-handed. Anyone who's worked in a busy kitchen knows that there are elements resembling an assembly line. All of the chefs and cooks must be able to perform under pressure, take and give orders clearly, shift tasks based on customer demand (you may not have budgeted enough burger toppings for the high school football team that came in early without a reservation), and much more.

Making it to the role-player stage may in many ways feel like a finish line. Trust us, it is far more of a start line than a finish line. Excel at this level and you will find yourself at the start line of another journey—the founder's journey. Find yourself on this journey and you will realize that your learning curve has only just begun.

If founders must come to the realization that their growth and development is never done, then all employees must also embrace the same reality. No one is above the team, no one is too good to improve, and no one gets to reach a point where they get to phone it in if they want to be successful.

While there may be distinct phases to the employee's journey, keep in mind that every journey is different. Some people may seem to coast through their journeys quickly. Don't get discouraged if your journey seems to be taking longer. It might mean you're meant to learn more and are being prepared for a bigger stage than someone you're comparing yourself against.

Comparing yourself to others is a recipe for misery. Your only competition should be against the you from yesterday. We don't know other people's full stories, so never compare yourself, or where you are on your journey, to others.

Lastly, more responsibility, and a fancier job title, don't always equal more money or more happiness. Life is a journey, the length of which is not guaranteed to anyone. The key to happiness at work, if you ask us, is to find meaning and joy in what you're doing right now and find compelling reasons to get better every day.

Your purpose, the vision you have for yourself, and your core values can go a long way in helping you find (or aligning with) those compelling reasons. Make your journey worth going on and it might just become one worth following.

References

1. Goldsmith, Marshall. *What Got You Here Won't Get You There*. 2007. Hyperion Books.

Chapter Eight

Employees: The Uphill Battle You Face

Below are just some of the actual sentiments we heard while administering our skills gap survey:

"I'm too old to handle the employee nonsense anymore. I just want to sell all of my businesses and focus on real estate."

"Yeah, we grew the business as hard and fast as we could and then we got the hell out of there before the people ate us alive."

"Human capital: the biggest asset and absolutely the biggest liability."

"If you have employees—you're going to have problems."

If you're coming into the workforce and think you're just going to show up and be greeted with open arms, you're wrong. Every organization already has momentum and likely a preconditioned bias against certain behaviours or skills. You need to consider the tens of thousands of candidates that came before you, and the small percentage of whom have done things correctly, and the large percentage who have taken short cuts.

This accumulation of experience influences how every action you make will be judged. These are the unintended consequences of entitled employees who expected a piece of the pie simply for showing up. Those who believed that because they wanted to lease a car, upgrade their cellular package or put a down payment on a condo, their employer should solve the problem by increasing their wages. Those who believed the time required to climb the corporate ladder was measured in weeks and months, rather than years and decades. Those who believe their rights were more important than providing quality service to the very people who paid the bills.

From our study of managers and business owners, the Top 3 deficiencies new candidates entering the workforce have are: communication, people skills and work ethic. We call these the "soft skills" but it's important to note that they aren't all created equal. While it's fantastic that everyone knows how to multi-task, communicate on multiple digital platforms, and is finely tuned in their work-life balance, the reality is there's a business to run that needs other skills more. Organizations rely on the combined efforts of many individuals ready, willing and able to row in the same direction. These skills are gained in relationship to other people and with repeated practice.

Here's another way to look at it. Hardware skills are easy to teach and learn—technical, tactical, mechanical in nature. But it's the software skills that are essential in differentiating the good from the great in business. These skills are hard to teach because you can't account for every single nuance and example that will present itself. These skills come from experience in doing. The more isolated we get, the more insular we become, the more difficult these skills are to develop. These skills are about complex decision-making, using our lifetime of experiences, not memorizing a theory or a singular process.

As a result, savvy entrepreneurs are trying to automate their businesses with technology by using technology and robots to replace the biggest potential assets and also the biggest liabilities in the workplace—humans. Technology is not emotional. It shows up and performs the task in the same manner, with the same degree of proficiency day in and day out. The business reality is this is what managers and owners rely on to be profitable and keep the doors open. From a customer standpoint, this offers consistency through their experience. Technology has few sick days, doesn't bring personal baggage into the professional workplace and seldom reports being undervalued and underappreciated for their work.

While this may sound like doom and gloom, it's the unfortunate reality. It's *your* reality. And with that let's get into our seven secret steps to help you become the exception.

1. Do your homework. The first thing you should do before deciding to get a job is to figure out the organization's vision, mission and values? Do they align with yours? Is it going to be a good fit? Take the time to research companies you think you're interested in working with. Search the Internet to find out about the ownership. What's their history? What experience do they have in the marketplace? Who is the manager? What are people saying about him or her? What is the list of goods being sold?

   For example, if you're applying for a job at a restaurant, ask questions ranging from what's the menu, all the way through to what's their charity of choice? Too many times people are showing up to organizations in which the vision, mission and values don't align and then wondering why they're not having a good experience. That's on you. Talk to past and present employees. What's their experience like? What were their highs and lows? What are the things that they think you should watch out for? Another idea is to show up and be the client—take in the entire experience. What's the vibe? What stands out? What do you notice? What things are people doing well, and what could be better? Does the price point match the value? Were you a satisfied client?

It's also important to understand what skills are required to excel at the job by doing your homework. Ask to intern. Think about all the time you wasted while in high school, college or university when you could have been deliberately interning at different jobs prior to showing up—trying them on for size during company time. Again, much like doing your homework, speaking to current and former employees is going to go a long way towards getting a good feel for what the organization can offer. Interning allows you to get up close and personal with the company culture. We need to move away from showing up to work places and trying on the job to see if it fits us. Doing our homework can immediately separate us from the uninformed 99 per cent.

2. Understand the difference between intellectual and emotional intelligence.

- Intellectual intelligence is the information that you glean from studying, memorizing and then regurgitating said information. Your mark or score is a reflection of how well you've retained that information. For years that number has been used as the indicator of your overall intelligence, and was essentially the only thing that prospective employers looked at as you entered the workforce. However, the reality in the workforce today is that everything is based on transactions. The quality of which is predicated on the foundation of trust. And this is where emotional intelligence comes in.

- Beth Barz defines emotional Intelligence as: self-awareness, self-management, social awareness and relationship management. Self-awareness is an introspective evaluation of how you present yourself to others. Are you tall and imposing or short, loud and persuasive? Shy or outgoing? Do you fight or embrace feedback? Are you combative and argumentative or submissive and agreeable? All important questions to ask yourself and be aware of prior to showing up in the workplace. Self-management takes it to the next level. How do you manage your strengths and areas of opportunity? Those you identified in Chapter 3.

  - Social awareness is about understanding the relationships, interactions and environment around you. What's acceptable and unacceptable? What's appropriate and inappropriate? What changes do you need to make to restore balance and harmony? And finally, how do you manage relationships? How are you at empathizing, listening, caring, sharing and building trust-based relationships? Spend time learning and understanding who you are. Who you *really are* versus who you think you are, or want to be.

- There is a difference in how you *want* to present yourself and how you *are* presenting yourself on a daily basis. Understand the impact that you have on people through your body language, mannerisms, tone, choice of words and actions. Too many people walk through life with a lack of self-awareness. It's often limiting to your personal and professional potential. We don't need to spend more time working on your hardware, that's the easy part. We need to spend time developing, installing and upgrading your software—emotional intelligence.

3. Get out and fail! It may be scary but it's a faster path forward. And the high school years are the perfect time to take chances on things you're not good at, or are outside of your comfort zone. Too many of us are sheltered from and/or avoid failure. We stick to our comfort zones and familiarity biases, which limits our scope of experience in the world. A world that really caters to a broad array of opportunities if we are brave enough to explore.

   Start small. Maybe it's volunteering to make dinner for your family or friends, sitting down to solve a puzzle or setting a budget for your own finances. The nature of tasks that you set out doesn't matter as long as they are outside of your normal day-to-day routine, comfort and skill set. Don't let other people help you out! Adopt the mindset that you're either winning or learning all the time. And understand that failure is an essential part of life and growth. There is no authentic victory without first working through adversity, and there is no adversity without first stepping up to a challenge.

The time to experiment is when you are young and have limited responsibilities. Your failure will impact your life and others' lives a lot less, so use this to your advantage. Remember, the stages of life: toddler, adolescent, teen, university, career, family. People often blow things up when they bring a high school attitude into their career stage of life. It's too late for that attitude to work or be tolerated by others, and the consequences are severe. Rest assured there's going to be plenty of learning and failing on the job, or a new environment, and you need to know how to respond perfectly. No book, pamphlet or podcast can replace the authentic experience of trying, failing and learning. Our parents and caregivers, while well intentioned, are actually holding us back by trying to flatten our adversity and preventing us from failing.

4. Know the pain points of business leadership. This is easy because we provided the Top 3 pain points in Chapter 2. Reminder, it's not what you know; it's what you do with what you know.

- Communication. The inability to articulate wants, needs or receive constructive feedback designed for the purpose of helping you maximize your work experience. It's not difficult to see why communication skills have dropped so vastly over the past decade. With the onset of technology, our preferred method of communication is through texts or likes, and the problem is, in the real world that's not what the customers want or need. In this setting, communication is the cornerstone of all human interaction and we need to learn how to become proficient communicators. If the golden rule is "Treat people how you'd like to be treated," then perhaps the golden rule of communication is "Speak to and listen to people as you would appreciate them doing for you."
- Work ethic is the ability to come to work and give 100 per cent of what you're capable of giving on that day for the mutually agreed upon time. Unfortunately, this generally accepted rule has steadily declined over the last 10 years. Perhaps because we're so used to having our parents and caregivers do things for us. And work ethic is something that is very difficult to teach because it is learned through example. Every young person should be ready, willing and able to put in a full eight-hour day, providing their best ability without distraction.

When did it become uncool to take pride in having a good work ethic? A good work ethic can quickly separate you from the crowd simply because it's become the exception rather than the norm. Much of this attitude speaks directly to the rise of the ego in modern society (the less evolved form of ourselves).

- Marketing slogans that tell you that you deserve the car, the trip, the cool clothes are preying on your lesser self and enticing you to make short-term, impulse decisions that harm you in the long-term. The antidote is learning to think further ahead. Earn it over the long run and purchase based on future goals instead of short-term desires. Put another way, everyone must *learn* to work hard. Some choose to embrace this reality, when they are young, sacrificing some luxuries or time with friends in order to create more opportunity and ease later in life. Others choose a life of ease, partying and spending every dollar they earn now, only to realize they need to work harder than they'd like, for fewer opportunities, later in life. Choose to work hard now. Leverage the time and energy you have right now. And watch how fast you get ahead!

- People skills. The ability to interact with, listen to, communicate with and serve others. A lot of this comes from self-awareness, which was secret step No. 2. These essential skills have also significantly decreased with the onset of technology. It's really easy to sit behind a computer screen and be a keyboard hero or heroine with a carefully worded, well researched email, but infinitely more difficult to communicate face-to-face, in real time. So how can you practise people skills? Some ideas might include a public speaking course like Toastmasters, speaking to others informally, being deliberate about asking questions, calling people versus texting, saying hello to people whose eyes meet yours as you're walking down the street, becoming more verbal in your circle of influence.
  - Whether it's communication, work ethic or people skills; just like anything else that we want to get good at, it takes time, practise, practise and more practise. We get to make the decision whether we're going to unplug ourselves from our devices, raise our heads and look around, make eye contact with people and have the courage and confidence to say hello. We need to decide whether we're going to show up to work, put our personal bias and issues aside, roll up our sleeves and strive to give

100 per cent. Choosing to push ourselves to do things we're uncomfortable with or find difficult is a reflection of how badly we really want to succeed. When we take ownership and admit our pain points, we start to understand that the decision to address them lies squarely on our shoulders.

5. Master the unwritten rules. There are a lot of unwritten rules in business and we're going to share our Top 3.

- Interviews matter. We all want to come to an interview prepared to shine, but how? Take the time to do the homework on the business: know their values, know their mission statement, know how long they've been in business, and know about their products. When you walk into the interview, put your phone away, greet people, ask questions.

  - When you arrive for the interview, don't sit down. Stand up and use the opportunity in the lobby, or in the seating area, to glean as much information as you can about different people. Ask the receptionist's name and introduce yourself. Introduce yourself to people you see walking in and out and observe what's happening in the workspace. Once in the interview, ask the interviewer how their day's going, what's new, and write down those answers. Dress appropriately. Create a resumé that stands out from everybody else. This is your time to shine, give it all you can. After the interview, the followup separates the "meh" from the "hell yeah I want this job!"

- When you're following up, remember the least effective and most effective ways of communicating. The least effective is email, more effective is the phone, and the most is face to face. Drop by the next day and answer any questions you couldn't the day before, and thank somebody for the interview. Tell the front desk receptionist you appreciated the opportunity. Adopt the 24-hour followup rule and you'll always stand out from the rest of the pack.

- The start time for any job is actually 15 minutes before the actual start time listed. If work starts at 8 a.m. that means it starts at 7:45 a.m. Business is beginning at 8 a.m., and you should already be there. A famous saying is if you're 10 minutes early, you're five minutes late. Get in the habit of giving yourself time to arrive, get prepared and be ready to rule when work begins. Leave your phone out of reach. In fact, leave all your personal belongings out of reach. Your manager, boss and coworkers aren't going to your house after work hours and peppering you with work questions and demands, so don't bring yours to their forum. Incidents of distraction have all but crippled the productivity of the modern workforce and if you're not prepared to go to work and fulfill the obligations that you've mutually agreed upon without distraction, then don't complain when you don't have a job.

- You will reap what you sow. Today too many people are trying to get things before they've invested any time, or energy, proving themselves. Prove yourself first so that you can legitimately ask for things later. Nowadays it's really, really easy to set yourself apart from the crowd without being entitled. We all know the trap most people fall into, because we live in an instantly gratified society that demands things now.

  - Be patient, delay your gratification until you've actually proven your value or your worth, and learn that the first year is not about you. The first year is all about you acclimating yourself to be a contributing member of the organization. And figuring out where you fit in. Save your breaks, finding good life-work balance, and time-off requests until you've proven your value to the organization. If you're capable of mastering our Top 3 unwritten rules of business, you're going to present yourself as the exception instead of the norm, and likely experience success beyond your wildest imagination.

6. Become a student of the game. The first thing you should do is understand that business operations are the simple economics of expenses versus profits. You want to be on the side that creates those profits. You want to be an asset, not a liability.

- Separate personal from professional at all times. Work is for work things and work people; your personal home life is for you and your people; when you mix the both you lose that work-life balance and there's nobody to blame but yourself.

- Master your personal literacies. We covered these in Chapter 3: values, strengths, opportunities, vision, mission, goals, objectives, guiding principles. These aren't a one-and-done thing. We're constantly reviewing, refining and adapting them to our present situation.

- Master your professional literacies. We talked about these in Chapter 4: feedback, communication, leadership, to name a few. The workplace is a living lab for improvement. It's also an opportunity to hone your personal and professional literacy skills.

- Level up your financial literacy. This was covered in Chapter 5: understand the difference between needs and wants, determine your financial goals and make plans to work towards them. Create your personal budget, stick to it and remember that time and patience go a long way.

- Don't fear asking questions. The worst questions are the ones that aren't asked. Never wing it, the risk is too big. Where possible, try to avoid asking the same question multiple times. Remember the scale of intelligence. Naive is making a mistake you didn't know was a mistake, stupid is making the same naive mistake twice, and ignorance is setting out to deliberately make a stupid mistake. We want to stay on the far end of that scale of intelligence.

- Do the little things well. Don't be above bending down to pick up garbage off the floor, or being the first to clean up a mess, organize a staff room and wash a dish. Remember success in life is a culmination of hundreds of thousands of little things done well every day.

- Understand that you are now part of a work ecosystem and everything that you do to preserve that ecosystem counts.

- Space it out. There's no need to attempt to start a new career, get married, put the down payment on the condo, buy the new truck, complete an online masters and achieve life balance at the same time. Do fewer things really well and allow yourself time to succeed.

- Work by the task and not by the clock. Don't be ruled by the clock; instead rule yourself by the desire to take pride in doing what you said you were going to do and when you said you were going to do it. Again, this is the quickest way to make yourself the exception and not the norm.

7. Be a lifelong learner. Understand that the older you get, the more you'll realize the less you know. And that's largely due to the rate of change in today's fast-paced society. But it's not only about what you need to learn, it's also what you need to unlearn. What was acceptable practice five years ago may not be acceptable today. Be conscious of that. Remember that until you're the manager, you need to respect that role. Too often people pass judgement without knowing what it's like to walk in someone else's shoes. Don't make assumptions. In fact, figure out how you can become an asset to that manager.

    The same goes with ownership. Until you're the owner, respect the owner—and all that the role entails. Don't be lulled into comparing your first, second and third year of showing up with 10, 20 and 30 years of building something from nothing, paying HR, opening bank accounts, signing off on agreements, creating codes of conduct, ensuring labour standards, paying CPP and EI, battling through lawsuits, balancing building a business with starting a family, and having to pivot with the realities of changing growth! And don't make the mistake of believing that tenure, or raises, are licences to start mailing it in. Think about the people that did that when you showed up and how it made you feel. Again the work environment is a delicate ecosystem with the cumulative success being the sum total of all its parts operating in harmony. Continue your education inside and outside of the industry.

Always, always, always look to be learning more. Read and listen to a book or a podcast at least every quarter. Select the topics or new technology that can help you enhance your skills and become more of an asset personally and professionally. These are easy wins, and this is how you use technology to your advantage instead of your detriment. Make yourself irreplaceable and at the same time keep the perspective that two weeks after you're gone customers will likely forget you were even there. Don't take it personally; it's just reality.

Articulate issues professionally, and only with those who can actually bring about desired results. Don't be the resident sounding board. And especially don't be the company complainer. Connect unhappy people to those who can make decisions. There's nothing worse than a cancer in the corporate culture, and anyone who's been successful in business understands that cancer must be removed at the first opportunity. And finally, when you leave for the day, leave it behind you. We've only got one life to live, and there isn't a sequel. We hear it time and time again. Those on their deathbeds aren't wishing they logged more hours at the office, made better contributions to the bottom line or stayed longer at work to get something completed. No, instead they're wishing they had spent more time and energy on the people who matter the most—themselves, their friends and their family.

Yes, this *is* your reality. Yes, it *is* an uphill battle. But we would rather prepare you for it than sugarcoat it. In the business world, there are winners and losers; not everybody gets a participation ribbon. You will make mistakes that you have to own, and there are no excuses, no parents or caregivers to defend you or explain why you weren't able to complete the task. This is real life and the hard work is ahead of you.

Theory into Practice: The Job Interview Preparation Checklist

Going into any job interview, you should always check the company's website, Google the company for any recent news (Did they just go through a merger? Did they just win an award of distinction, or was the CEO just on the news?), and check their social media links (often found at the top or bottom of their website homepage). In doing so, you should have written down, and ideally memorized:

- ❑ Company purpose (why they exist; often found under the About Us, Company History, Our Story or Values sections)
- ❑ Core Values
- ❑ Operating territory (are they a local, national or worldwide company?)
- ❑ Key products and services (what do they do?)
- ❑ Customer base (who do they serve?)
- ❑ Key personnel (know who's on the team, including board of directors if applicable)
- ❑ Any recent big news (could be on found on website, Google, or social media)
- ❑ People you may have in common (find out who is interviewing you, check their LinkedIn profile and see what connections you may have in common—this could be a good icebreaker, and a way to build familiarity and trust faster)

Theory into Practice: Self and Peer Mini-Assessment

Self/ Peer Mini-Assessment

Top Strengths, Behaviours or Traits

1. _____

_____

2. _____

_____

3. _____

_____

4. _____

_____

5. _____

_____

6. _____

_____

7. _____

_____

8. _____

_____

Comments:

Top opportunities for development or improvement/ blind spots

1. _____

_____

2. _____

_____

3. _____

_____

4. _____

_____

5. _____

_____

Comments:

Note: When assessing your own behaviour, or asking others to, please remember/ ask your peers to:

- Be specific
- Give you the straight goods without too much explanation or justification
- Give examples where possible
- When polling your peers, quantify your responses above so you can detect trends

Theory into Practice: Personal Development Plan

Personal Development Plan

Key Outcome	Strategy/ Plan	Resources/ Barriers	Success Measure/ Date
Ex. Learn to code	- Take online coding course - Try small "beta project" for company intranet	$300, need supervisor approval	Course done by next April, beta project by June

Life Literacies

1. Due to the social landscape, there are inherent challenges you will face when entering the workforce. The better educated you are about those challenges, the better equipped you will be.

2. Do your homework prior to showing up at a job. Ideally, you seek alignment with your personal and professional values.

3. Understand the difference between EQ and IQ. Books smarts are not linearly correlated with street smarts. Street smarts are valuable.

4. You're either winning or learning. Don't embrace failure as a negative, and try to fail early and often when you are young and supported.

5. Learn and master the unwritten rules of the business. You'll get out of the experience what you chose to invest into it.

6. Becomes a student of the game. Learn the ins and outs of the business operations so you can become an irreplaceable asset.

7. Commit to becoming a lifelong learner. The more you know ,the more you can grow personally and professionally.

Chapter Nine

Employers: The Uphill Battle You Face

Today's businesses are like a lightning-fast machine. A machine in perpetual motion that simply cannot pause for their teams' development needs. Employee turnover, business continuity challenges, customer dissatisfaction, and attrition can all be attributed to a breakdown in an organization's talent level or the attitude of the team.

Having worked with over a hundred different organizations in our coaching business, the linkage between organizational culture, talent development and financial performance is beyond clear (Figure 2.1, Chapter 2). The employers of today and the leaders of tomorrow must walk a delicate tightrope between creating and protecting a healthy organizational culture, developing the skills of

125

tomorrow and tolerating mistakes while setting a high bar for performance.

If the workforce of tomorrow faces an uphill battle in encountering and overcoming adversity, developing desirable skills and learning at a breakneck pace, then the employer of tomorrow faces a veritable Mount Everest.

Leaders don't have the option to phone it in. Leaders are most needed in times of chaos, conflict and confusion, and most organizations are about to dive into all three. We're all trying to pivot in some way and develop teams for a complicated and uncertain future. This is compounded by the fact that since the global economic crisis of 2008, and continued economic destabilization, executives in senior leadership positions and other desirable jobs are staying in the posts longer. They are retiring later, which means fewer years of "time in the saddle" for the next wave. Decades of experience must, in extreme cases, be replaced by months of experience. Furthermore, with the ever-more-popular mandate to "do more with less," under-resourced teams have documented less and less of their systems. This means more of what it takes to be successful lives in Sheila's head, and when Sheila retires, Brian gets to start not with a leg up, but exactly where Sheila did. New employees have less knowledge handed down, but with sometimes razor-thin profits, mistakes are less likely to be forgiven. Make a costly mistake in business today? You're likely to receive the business equivalent of being taken behind the barn and shot.

There is also another systemic challenge that leaders must face. If schools cannot fail students even for not doing the work, and parents perpetuate their children's "fragile snowflake" ego by telling them that they are amazing at everything, regardless of performance, then all roads lead to the employer as the first person who must give negative or unpleasant feedback to young people. Not fun. Mental health challenges are already rising at an unprecedented rate, employee turnover is up, loyalty is down, and the window of opportunity for employers to shape the workforce of tomorrow in a meaningful way is becoming increasingly smaller.

Leaders need to put on their hard hats. Referring back to our construction analogy, companies that win in the marketplace of the future will create better blueprints. If culture is the foundation of the skyscraper, and skills are the floors you see above ground, then an integrated organizational strategy that prioritizes culture, talent development and profit is akin to the blueprints all construction is predicated upon.

We have always advocated that organizational culture is either built by design or by default. Organizational cultures that are built by design have a clear and compelling vision, well-articulated core values that are alive in every aspect of the organization, and an actionable mission statement that integrates its way into every aspect of the overarching strategy.

Organizational cultures that are built by default are often created when undesired behaviours are tolerated while the rest of the company is too busy pursuing profit. In this instance, the behaviours grow organically and manifest as an accumulation of what leadership is willing to tolerate. With no push back from leadership or a unified direction, the loudest voice wins and the squeaky wheel gets the grease. Rarely is the default culture in the team's best long-term interest. It's usually the "bad locker room" influence or the organizational cancer mentioned earlier.

In short, the first line of defence, or the earliest opportunity for success for a future-thinking organization, is to be laser-focused, deliberate and consistent when it comes to setting and maintaining their organizational culture. With the right people and the right plan, the right leaders can move mountains. If the wrong people are allowed into the organization and given a say, all of the planning in the world can still end up in catastrophe.

The second critical survival and success factor for tomorrow's workforce is an implementation strategy for accelerated talent development. Talent development, upskilling and other forms of employee enrichment can no longer be viewed as perks. They are a *must*. Teaching skills needs to evolve into *imparting* skills. What's the difference? Well, theoretical knowledge will no longer cut it, organizations need to *show* not just *tell* employees what to do. The name of the game in tomorrow's business landscape will be practical application.

In the age of social media, the Internet, Blockchain, artificial intelligence and more disruption than continuity, today's workplace must have a clear understanding of their collective strengths and opportunities if they are to leverage an effective talent development program.

Therefore, the third staple of their success is organizational self-awareness. Regular positive and constructive feedback, coaching, performance reviews and other self- and peer-based assessments are a prerequisite to understanding individual and collective development needs in order to accurately prioritize talent development initiatives. If an organization doesn't know the strengths and opportunities of their leaders and team members, how would they possibly choose which skills to focus on? If they don't understand how, as an organization, they are prone to disruption, how can they craft defensible business strategies?

We look at it this way; the organization of tomorrow must be self-aware, and the successful leaders of tomorrow must be humble. They may believe they have been right nearly all of their career, yet they must resist the urge to surround themselves with "yes people," and instead hire for differences and diversity of thought and talent.

If young professionals are to be taught to enter the workforce humble, hungry, hard-working and open to feedback and learning, then those charged with leading the next wave must model these behaviours. If the next generation is approaching work with a truculent, hesitant attitude, then leaders must realize that today's typical young employee doesn't respond to "Do what I say, not what I do," or "This is just how things work around here."

In short, the young people entering our workplaces today have very little tolerance for B.S. and hypocrisy!

Life Literacies

1. Culture eats strategy for breakfast. If your strategy is the "what" you are trying to accomplish, then your culture is how your team goes about it. Success is far more dependent on execution than it is the battle plans.

2. The pace of change is accelerating. Those with the best jobs are retiring later. This means the learning curve must be steeper, and the "runway" (expected time to competency) for new hires must be much shorter.

3. Many young people have been told they are unique, special, perhaps even perfect their whole lives. We have created a generation that can't handle feedback or adversity. Given the problems mentioned above that we're about to throw them into, we are doing a terrible job of equipping our young people for success as parents, teachers, coaches and early employers.

4. Companies that intentionally and rigorously focus on culture and profit will financially outperform their counterparts. Companies that win in the future will prioritize their value proposition and their people development.

5. Companies must become self-aware in terms of their strengths and their gaps. The only way to

have self-aware companies is to have self-aware leaders who seek out feedback, growth and new knowledge.

6. Great news for any parent reading this book: the best way to prepare your children for these challenges is to do less! By coddling them, or *saving* them from adversity, you are actually crippling your children, preventing them from developing resiliency by overcoming one challenge at a time.

Chapter Ten

Leaders: Lead, Follow or Get Out of the Way

While we have addressed our incoming future leaders for most of this book thus far, we now turn to our most senior business, community, and organizational leaders, as they are an important part of leading the changes that must be made.

Dear business owners and CEOs, what would you give to know what you didn't know when starting your business journey? Would you do almost anything to avoid "learning on your own dime"—often to the tune of tens or hundreds of thousands of dollars along the way?

After more than two decades leading our own businesses, and advising other start-ups, we would have given *a lot* to understand the ins and outs, ups and downs of business beforehand. Specifically, we would have wanted to see what lay ahead from the perspective of our personal growth. It was through this lens, and the experience of helping over 250 small, medium, and large businesses identify their growth opportunities through our consulting company that we've identified the four stages entrepreneurs must pass through en route to becoming truly remarkable business leaders. This is what the future is demanding of leaders—*now*.

Let's begin the founders' journey.

Owner/ Operator

There are few things in life more exciting than beginning your entrepreneurial journey. You've identified a gap or market trend (possibly even a new market) and you have an idea. You've spent sleepless nights wondering if your idea is legit. You've done your due diligence, market analysis, and culled the wisdom of your entrepreneurial tribe. And just like that, you are open for business with a minimum viable product. What. A. Rush!

The founder's first role: owner / operator. The job description is simple: Do everything. Budgets are tight, expenses must not exceed revenue and there's only 24 hours in a day to make, sell, market, and improve your product or service. You're the graphic designer, receptionist, head of sales and product development. You're the chief deliverer of the service, manufacturer of the widget, bookkeeper, human resources manager, lead recruiter, and you are the customer service agent. Regardless of the request, the answer is "that's me" and this continues to the point where three things happen:

1. The demand for your service or product outpaces your ability to keep up.
2. You begin to lose energy from going 24/7 – 365.
3. First hires feel a glass ceiling and leave in search of greater autonomy and opportunity.

At this point in time, you come to the realization that scaling any organization requires three commodities besides cash that you never seem to have enough of.

1. Time
2. Energy
3. Patience

You've willed your business to grow and hired with a "just watch me and do what I do" process and now you're wondering why your team isn't delivering the same level of service, with the same level of enthusiasm as you. This is your first founder's revelation; you cannot scale without creating buy-in. It turns out, "buy-in" is an exercise in trust over a lengthy, intentional process that requires a plan. No plan, no purpose, no point. We've seen it, done it and lived it. The improvement pathway looks like this:

1. Build it
2. Sell it
3. Deliver it (product or service)
4. Ask and learn about it
5. Repeat one through four

6. Scale it

A founder of a new business who remains at the owner/operator tier of their development for a prolonged period of time is often described as having bought themselves a full-time job. If you asked a dozen founders how many sought to buy themselves a job, the response is zero. No founder plans to bottleneck themselves, which is why we must all learn along the way.

To escape this fate, it's critical for leaders to understand how to transition from acting as an owner/ operator to becoming a capable manager.

Manager

Success is a system and more often than not, that system need not be re-invented as much as it need be implemented. In our experience, the three most constraining forces limiting business growth are:

- Cash flow
- Time
- The "inner-game" of the founder (their learning curve, focus, attitude, and perspective)

The founder's inner-game is the subject of every self-help, personal success, leadership, or coaching resource on the planet. For the sake of simplicity, let's treat time and cash as resources to be managed carefully in order to maximize a return on their investment.

To effectively manage human, time and capital resources within a growing business, a founder must intermittently pause participating "in the business" and begin to observe their business with a focus on improvement (let's call this being "on the business"). In short, founders must take out their proverbial clipboards and:

- Perform a process audit/ gap analysis
- Create, implement, and teach one system at a time
- Audit what they've implemented (annually/ sporadically)
- Measure it (daily/ weekly/ monthly/ quarterly, yearly)
- Hold their team accountable to standards
- Create a non-ambiguous "one-size-fits-all" approach their customers, team and potential investors can understand

Most management tenures begin with the same three questions:

1. What are the organizational gaps?
2. What processes do we need to put in place to manage them?
3. How do we evaluate the effectiveness of these processes?

Next, one of two management styles typically manifests:

1. The firefighter. Management attempts to address every issue at the same time (putting out fires

everywhere), overwhelming the workplace with change demands and little evolutionary progress occurs.

2. The bricklayer. Management creates, implements, and teaches one system at a time, which helps build alignment, understanding. Systematic growth occurs through consistent desired behaviour.

Slow and steady wins the race. Each new system must be carefully introduced and audited on a consistent basis in order to gage effectiveness. Only after the majority have become proficient with the new system should an additional system be introduced.

Managers must understand that success in any system requires holding people accountable. People love the notion of accountability until the point where it's *them* in the hot seat, so it's important for the founder to over-communicate the *why* of the organization as the beacon all members must be focused on. Any leader who over-communicates the *what* is going to be met with one question: *Why*? Aligning purpose with systems and strategy is akin to aligning heart and mind, and that defines the next stage in a founder's journey.

Leader

Recall that a manager is charged with maximizing efficiency and increasing the likelihood of business survival through being an effective steward of company resources. While it seems popular to bash management and glorify leadership, both are essential. After all, rah-rah speeches lose their effect if you're not sure if your company will be around tomorrow. That being said, humans don't act like ants or robots for long. As soon as their minds have been conditioned to act in unison, their hearts cry out to act in unique or even rebellious ways. After all, how many business icons inspired you by going to school, getting a job, getting married, and putting in their 35 years without rocking the boat?

While managers try to create a "one-size-fits-all" approach, leaders take a "one-size-fits-one" approach to achieve greater buy-in one team member at a time. Like parenting, it can often be a thankless job. Fortunately, a founder who was successfully able to grow into the shoes of a manager does not have to transition into leadership from step zero. They've already picked up new skills along the way.

Remember, you started your business for a reason that was bigger than you. With a profound *why* the team can get behind, and standards of accountability to the individual, team, and organization, it is easier to create buy-in. Thus, the task of management becomes simpler when leaders can take the time to understand what motivates, and what matters to, each team member. We often call this the "currency" of the individual.

Any founder knows that cash is oxygen for any business. The leader's job is to bridge the gap between the currency of the individual and that of the organization. If managers are in the efficiency business, then leaders are in the alignment business.

Leaders must not only be self-aware; they must also be "socially aware" as described by Bradberry and Greaves in their book *Emotional Intelligence 2.0*. In this context, social awareness is being able to read situations, and the emotional states of all of the players involved, to develop effective go-forward strategies.

Lastly, while managers understand capacity, leaders must understand capability and character. Leaders understand that while output is essential to measure, there is a bigger picture. No team member, regardless of talent, can be tolerated if they are a toxin to the larger entity. Furthermore, it's possible to be on the right team but playing the wrong role. Leaders look beyond productivity and see potential.

In short, while managers strive to reach output potentials, leaders work to unleash the latent potential of their teams. Few founders reach this level of inspiring leadership, and so how could there possibly be yet another step in the evolution of a founder? Well, we all need goals to aspire to. Plus, we bet the competitor in you is already yearning to beat the odds and make it to our elusive fourth stage!

Mentor

If you've worked hard enough, and worked enough on yourself, to truly become a leader, then your organization is better for it. The problem is, your organization likely isn't the same without you, which is a problem for anyone who might want to buy your business, and it's a problem for you if you ever want to retire and not leave a ghost town behind you.

The fact is, there needs to be one last step in the founder's evolution—a scenario in which their organization thrives without them. Paraphrasing John Maxwell, true leaders produce other leaders who produce other leaders.

In essence, mentors cultivate an organizational culture that transcends the business, and the people who are in it today. Mentors focus beyond the bottom line in their decision-making. True mentors know that by growing those in their care to the best of their ability, some will spread their wings and leave the nest, but not before making the nest better for others first.

If owners are in the vision business, managers are in the efficiency business and leaders are in the alignment business, then mentors are in the sustainability business.

On most days:

- Owners ask, "What's going to work?"
- Managers ask, "Who and what isn't working?"
- Leaders ask, "What are we really building here?" and "Are we living our values and culture?"
- Mentors ask, "How can I be of service?"

On their worst days:

- Owners ask, "How can I make money?"
- Managers ask, "How can I make more money?"
- Leaders ask, "How can I keep my best people around?"
- Mentors ask, "How can I grow more people?"

On their best days:
- Owners ask, "How can I change the world?"
- Managers ask, "How can I improve things so we have a better chance of changing the world?"
- Leaders ask, "What does my team need from me to achieve the mission?"
- Mentors ask, "How am I in the way of progress?"

Just like not every founder will enjoy a unicorn $1-billion exit, not every founder will become a mentor who changes the world. No founder can survive without being intimately aware of what is working and not working in their business and adapting quickly to serve changing markets. The business icons we all read about, study and admire, apply the same lens of improvement to themselves.

While it may seem simple when laid out in four logical, progressive stages, business is hard. Challenges are ever-present, and there will always be an excuse not to work on yourself because you're too busy giving the business what it needs. What's important for every founder is to ask themselves is if they are truly satisfied where they are. Or if their vision—and their identity of who they must become—is calling them to more. Do you want to make money in a lifestyle business? Do you want to create opportunities for others? Or do you want to change the world?

Your goals should dictate your growth, and if your ego can get out of the way, anything is possible.

Theory into Practice: The Four Stages of a Founder's Journey

Owner/ Operator	Manager	Leader	Mentor/ Coach
Have a vision (see the gap/ market trend/ new market/ better world)	Critical analysis (process audit/ gap analysis)	The "wait-a-minute" question: "what are we *really* doing/ building here?"	The "successor-ship" question "how can this grow without me?"
Understand the problem (due diligence, market analysis)	Create, implement and teach one system at a time	Understand it	Bequeath it (empower those who empower those who build it, market it, sell it, record it)
Create an MVP	Audit it (annually/ sporadically)	Competency analysis (skill/ attitude gap analysis)	
Improvement cycle	Measure it (daily/ weekly/ monthly/ QTR)	Understand us (who's really on our team—passion/ skills/ story)	Challenge it ("I see your potential, and that is what I will demand from you, but I'll coach you to get there")
-Build it	Hold people accountable to standards		
-Sell it	"one-size-fits-all" approach	The "authenticity" question: "are we living our vision and values?"	
-Deliver it (product or service)			"one-world" approach (growing people beyond our walls is good for them and good for the world, and that alone is good for us)
-Ask and learn about it		Move it (right people on/ off bus—into the right seats)	
-Repeat one through four		Align it (individual/ organizational success)	
-Scale it		Unleash it (inspire the latent discretionary effort of the team)	
"one-solution-fits-all" approach		"one-size-fits-one" approach	

Life Literacies

1. Self-awareness and personal growth aren't just for employees. Arguably these concepts are even more important for leaders.

2. Leaders are often the single biggest bottleneck in business. Rather than blame your team (who might need a lot of personal and professional development), look in the mirror and look to improve yourself first.

3. Leaders have four distinct phases to their professional journey, which are defined by different skills and different ways of bringing value to the organization.

4. Getting better at what you do is a "rest-of-your-life" project.

Resources

1. Bradberry, Travis & Greaves, Jean. 2009. *Emotional Intelligence 2.0*. TalentSmart.

Chapter Eleven
Building the Resilient Organization of the Future

What's the first step to building the organization of the future? And how do organizations address the competency gaps we've addressed in this book so far? Future-ready organizations first need to develop effective talent evaluation and assessment criteria at both the individual and organizational levels. It would be difficult, potentially even wasteful, for any organization to deploy training and development without this first step.

We've used a few building analogies in the previous chapters, but let's shift the final analogy to something more organic. Many business leaders today refer to their organization as a living, breathing entity. We love that concept because, at the end of the day, business is all about the people in it. To build a living, breathing entity that can withstand the challenges employers face today, we suggest the following anatomical structure.

The Heart

The heartbeat of any organization is its organizational culture. The purpose, core values and mission of the organization collectively serve as the heart. Metaphorically, the heart pumps blood to the rest of the body, just as an organization's culture makes its way into every facet of business life. We all know that a human heart performs better with regular exercise and so does the heart of the organization. It becomes far more effective when the core values, purpose and mission are built into every intricacy, system and even meeting that you have.

The Brain

The cerebral aspects of any business, or team, are the strategic components.

- Go-to-market strategy
- Value proposition
- Source(s) of competitive differentiation
- Intellectual property or any proprietary aspects of the business
- The strategic plan
- Innovation and disruptive ideas
- Recruitment, onboarding and training strategies

The Lungs

It's been said many times that cash is oxygen for any business, and so it is. The economics of the business (cash flow strategies, accounting and budgeting) keep oxygen flowing to the rest of the body, which is crucial for survival. Any individual contributor, who hopes to have a job for the foreseeable future, should know how the work they do helps keep the lights on and oxygen flowing!

The Liver

In the human body, the liver is the primary organ responsible for detoxification—removing harmful substances from the bloodstream. The corporate answer to the liver is an organization's people and culture department and strategy. Often falling under the human resources umbrella, a well-functioning HR department keeps an organization's culture healthy in the same way that the liver keeps all bodily tissues healthy, removing toxic influences as soon as they are detected. Furthermore, a great HR department acts as a gatekeeper. They prevent the wrong influences from entering the system in the first place.

Musculoskeletal System

In the human body, movement is made possible by our bones, ligaments and muscles (collectively referred to as our musculoskeletal system). The business equivalent of the musculoskeletal system is the team. After receiving an electrical impulse from the brain, all the bones and muscles have to work together in order to produce meaningful movement. Similarly, after receiving the strategy from the leadership of an organization, the team must work collectively in order to maximize their collective performance and opportunities. Just as the more one invests in their physical health through exercise, the more the muscles grow stronger and more capable; the more an organization invests in their team, the more capable they become.

Taken one step further, the legs are akin to the quality of the systems an organization adopts, and how consistently the team executes them. In both cases we won't get very far without them.

GPS Watch

Just as a smart watch like a Garmin, or Apple watch equipped with GPS, can help us monitor our body's function and reach our destination, a strong dashboard helps a business get where it needs to go. A company dashboard is comprised of relevant metrics, or KPIs (key performance indicators), that serve as litmus tests to help the team understand how they are performing relative to benchmark performance criteria. A great dashboard adds rigour to strategy by informing where more or less effort is required. Examples of key metrics that the high-performance organization of the future may want to pay close attention to are:

- Employee retention rates
- Employee engagement
- Customer satisfaction

- Absenteeism
- Use of sick days, and costs associated with sick leave and use of benefits (an overworked or highly disengaged team becomes a heavy financial burden)
- Cost of Customer Acquisition (CoA) compared to Customer Lifetime Value (CLV); sometimes expressed as CLV/ CoA
- Sales pipeline and sales pipeline/ deal flow by team member
- Training and continuing education costs
- Cultural entropy (assessed via surveys such as those performed by the Barrett Values Centre; basically how much energy is working *against* the organization)
- Core competency measures (not definable or measurable for every job)
- Time to competency (i.e. from time a new skill is taught to demonstration of acceptable standards)

When viewed through this lens, the resilient organization of the future has a backdrop with which to assess incoming talent, existing gaps, and from there can develop recruitment, development and ongoing training plans.

As one of the top leadership experts and executive coaches of our time, Dr. Marshall Goldsmith, suggests in his bestseller *What Got You Here Won't Get You There*, even if the best practices you utilized helped you become successful, organizations that aspire to survive and thrive amidst their new reality must be open, if not eager, to change.

The resilient organization of the future will be self-aware and adaptable. The organizations that will win the new talent war will attract, develop and retain the best talent. They will know how to measure what matters, develop or hire the right capabilities, and adapt as needs and competency gaps emerge. A "but this is the way we've always done it" attitude in organizations will be an invitation for the best talent to find work elsewhere.

Just as the parents, teachers and coaches of tomorrow need to learn to allow their youth to encounter and learn from adversity sooner and more often, the organization that hopes to emerge victorious in today's business climate cannot bury its head in the sand. People are a complex, imperfect and unpredictable lot, so your people strategy has to be anything but fixed. It must grow.

Great leadership is not a position of power or influence. We would argue that true leadership is a call to service. By this definition (if not by common sense), leadership is not for everyone. We advocate for systemic, if not societal solutions, to better prepare our youth. The consequences of not supporting young people ultimately impacts all of us.

This is our call to arms for all leaders to show up more than you ever have. To be more than you ever have. To serve more than you ever have. You got into leadership for a reason. If it was simply money and power, we collectively ask you to vacate your position to make way for real leaders. If it was to make an impact, we have good news for you—now's your time, and now's your chance. Our youth need you, and the world needs great leaders now more than ever.

This is our call to action for the next generation. We, as your predecessors, have failed you in many ways. We have made mistakes. As your parents, we tried to protect you from harm because we love you, but we realize protecting you yesterday crippled you today from dealing with the adversity you must face to become an adult in your own right. Forgive us. More importantly, find the competitive spirit within you to rise up to the challenges life is throwing you, and prove your naysayers wrong. Prove us wrong. Forget entitlement, convenience and ease. Show us grit, teamwork and long-term commitment. Do that, and the keys to the kingdom are yours.

Employers...

New employees...

Show us what you're made of!

Acknowledgments

This book would not be possible were it not for a lot of support from others. First and foremost, thank you to our families for the support, encouragement and perspective you offer each of us as we go about our hectic schedules and zany pursuits trying to change the world for the better.

Thank you to everyone who participated in our skills gap survey, and thank you to every entrepreneur, executive and business leader we interviewed as we tested and validated our theories.

Thank you to our editor Jacqueline Honnet, and thank you to Hot Soup Media for our cover design that we so love! We cannot thank the team at Morgan James publishing enough for the support, guidance, and collaborative and supportive process! Right from Founder David Hancock to Publisher Jim Howard, Publishing Director Bethany Marshall, our Author Relations Manager Gayle West, and the entire author support and publishing team— working with you has been a dream. Thank you for sharing our vision for *Life Literacy*!

Thank you to Marshall Goldsmith and John Mattone for your mentorship as two of the world's top executive coaches, and Marshall for your amazing testimonial! Thank you to Nails Mahoney, Nick Roud, Summer Smith, John G Miller, and Michael O'Donnell for your tremendous endorsements and your friendship!

Lastly, thank you to every client we have ever worked with, every team member we have worked beside, and every business partner we've had during our careers. Our collective journeys have been thousands of lessons from each of you combined. Everything we learned to be able to teach anything has been a gift, so thank you from the bottom of our hearts!

About the Authors

Nelson Soh is a certified numbers Guru and an entrepreneur. He is a Chartered Accountant (now referred to as Chartered Professional Accountant) and a University of British Columbia, Sauder School of Business graduate who brings a wealth of knowledge from a diverse experience background. Nelson started his career as an external auditor in public practice working with publicly traded companies, private small businesses, not-for-profit and government organizations.

After transitioning out of public practice, Nelson has worked with a wide variety of companies including a:

- Fortune 1000 company
- SKYTRAX Top 5 globally ranked airline
- Industry-leading premium fitness franchise
- Canada-wide healthcare company
- Tech company that forefronts the experimentation and website optimization industry
- Global leader in the education and learning industry

One of Nelson's biggest strengths is in helping people understand money and finances in a simple and easy to understand way. With a passion for helping others paired with his expertise and experience in finance and accounting, Nelson shares his knowledge around financial literacy through various social media platforms as a way to help people avoid common pitfalls and pave their way to financial freedom.

Since becoming a CPA, Nelson has shared his knowledge through speaking engagements, was featured on the CPA BC website, and guest spoken on multiple podcasts. Nelson has also written multiple articles around personal finance for the CPA Canada and other businesses.

To give back to the community, Nelson volunteers his time by mentoring young adults and professionals who are starting their careers and is a member on a board of advisors for a local college in Vancouver.

In 2020, Nelson launched his first personal finance online course, a "Beginner's Guide to Managing Money," through an online learning platform. This course teaches some fundamental principles around money that most people are not formally taught. The course has over 150 students enrolled around the globe and continues to grow today.

A believer that mindset is everything; Nelson has taken the first step to help others improve their *money mindset* by creating the "100-Day Money Mindset Journal." A 100-Day guided journal to develop a stronger, more positive money mindset that will unlock your unlimited potential to attract money into your life.

Nelson is active on LinkedIn, Facebook, Instagram (@ nelsonsoh_), and Twitter.

More about Nelson can be found at www.nelsonsoh. com

Matt **Young** is an Ernst & Young Entrepreneur of the Year finalist, Business in Vancouver and Caldwell Partners Canadian Top 40 Under 40 business award winner. This serial entrepreneur graduated with a Kinesiology Degree from the University of British Columbia and started his first start-up company, a boutique health & fitness business: Innovative Fitness. Matt's ability to distill complex constructs into bite-sized pieces that can be understood and activated by those delivering the service and the consumer has made him a sought-after business consultant. Matt has worked with numerous small- and medium-sized businesses ranging from Deloitte, to Velofix, to Habitat for Humanity around creating solid foundations upon which future success can be built.

After scaling his fitness business into a franchise, Matt sold in 2018 and turned his attention to supporting a variety of for-profit and not-for-profit organizations in the health, wellness and sport sector at the local, national and international levels. These organizations include;

- British Columbia Children's Hospital Live 5-2-1-0 initiative
- British Columbia Physical Literacy Alliance
- Alberta Physical Literacy Alliance
- Canada's Physical Literal Alliance
- Norwegian Sport Federation
- The National Hockey League
- The Lichtenstein Olympic Committee
- The United States Olympic Committee
- The PGA of America

- Canada Soccer
- Ontario, British Columbia & New Brunswick Soccer
- Tennis, Ringette, Rugby, Softball and Cycling British Columbia

Matt is the Founder of the Quality Coaching Collective www.qcoachingcollective.com and the Quality Sport Hub www.qualitysporthub.com. He is regularly engaged by sport parents, coaches and administrators to help navigate the complexities in the youth sport system. Matt has published numerous articles for magazines and journals, has authored and published seven books, and with the support of his team, raised over $6.1 million and counting for community charity, including a seven-day Guinness World Record bike relay across Canada that raised over $1 million for Juvenile Diabetes Research.

A strong believer that culture trumps process, Matt is the example of walking the talk and living your values. He is the Co-Founder of the Just Go Play Podcast https://www.justgoplay.ca/ which connects industry leaders with recreational athletes, parents and coaches in support of his personal mantra; as many as possible, as long as possible, in the best environments possible.

Matt is active on Twitter and LinkedIn and can be reached through those platforms.

Stan **Peake** lives to lift others towards their potential. In the process of becoming obsessed with helping others discover and strive toward their potential, Stan's story is more "school of hard knocks" than Ivy League MBA.

After an 18-year career in the health, fitness and medical industries that saw Stan own his first two businesses (including a buyout of his second business venture), Stan turned his passion of coaching others from fitness journeys to coaching leaders and entrepreneurs in their business and career pursuits.

After breaking his back in a mountain biking accident just three months after leaving his previous business, Stan was able to grow his coaching practice, InSite Performance Coaching, into a national firm with clients across Canada, the United States and Europe; with coaches in Vancouver, Calgary and Toronto.

Certified as an Executive Coach by the world's No. 1 Executive Coach John Mattone (former coach to Steve Jobs), Stan is also certified as a corporate facilitator. Rounding out Stan's certifications are his certification in deploying 360-degree peer reviews, and his certification in cultural transformation tools.

Stan holds a graduate certificate in values-based leadership from Royal Roads University in Victoria, BC, as well as an executive education in sales leadership from Queens University in Ontario. Stan now shares his experiences as a guest lecturer at Mount Royal University in Calgary, AB.

Stan is also a serial entrepreneur, with ownership experience in seven businesses to date.

Life Literacy is Stan's sixth book, and three of his previous books reached bestseller status (*How to Sell in Any Economy, Success is a System*, and *Now What? 50 ways to build your business in a crisis*). Stan has also been published in many national newspapers, several magazines including *Entrepreneur*, and has appeared as a guest on over 20 podcasts on topics ranging from entrepreneurism to psychology to principles of success.

When not coaching entrepreneurs or executives, writing his next book, or giving his latest keynote speech, Stan enjoys travelling, exercise and spending time with his friends, and his wife Maria, son Chase and dog Zeke. While his business takes him across North America and beyond, Stan resides with his family in Calgary, Alberta, Canada.

Stan can be reached at stan@insiteperformancecoaching.com and is also active on LinkedIn.

A free ebook edition is available with the purchase of this book.

To claim your free ebook edition:

1. Visit MorganJamesBOGO.com
2. Sign your name CLEARLY in the space
3. Complete the form and submit a photo of the entire copyright page
4. You or your friend can download the ebook to your preferred device

A **FREE** ebook edition is available for you or a friend with the purchase of this print book.

CLEARLY SIGN YOUR NAME ABOVE

Instructions to claim your free ebook edition:
1. Visit MorganJamesBOGO.com
2. Sign your name CLEARLY in the space above
3. Complete the form and submit a photo of this entire page
4. You or your friend can download the ebook to your preferred device

Print & Digital Together Forever.

Snap a photo

Free ebook

Read anywhere